# Reflections on China's Road to Development

## Nine Essays by Hu Sheng, 1983 – 1996

*by*

Hu Sheng（胡绳）

English Translation by Liu Ruixiang, Paul White et al.
Revised by Suzan Dewar

The Commercial Press
Beijing

ISBN 7-100-02447-1
I. Modern China — History     II. Hu Sheng

Published by The Commercial Press
36 Wang Fu Jing Street, Beijing 100710, China

Printed in the People's Republic of China

was published in the former Soviet Union, the former German Democratic Republic, Uruguay and Japan in the respective languages of these countries. Its English and Korean language editions were published in Beijing. Over three million copies of *From the Opium War to the May Fourth Movement* were published in China. Its English edition was published in Beijing. His major essays, theses and representative works now appear in *The Complete Works of Hu Sheng* of approximately three million words scheduled to be published in 1997.

# CONTENTS

Hu Sheng (in 1996)

# THE AUTHOR

Hu Sheng was born in January 1918 in Suzhou of Jiangsu Province. He attended middle school in Suzhou and Shanghai and after graduation enrolled in the Peking University in 1934. Starting from the latter half of 1935, he tutored himself while writing in Shanghai and took part in the cultural activities led by the Chinese Communist Party (CCP). He joined the CCP in Wuhan in January 1938. From the end of the 1930s to the 1940s he was chief editor and editor of a number of newspapers and journals. He also worked in several local CCP leading organs in the cultural field. After the founding of the People's Republic of China, he was secretary-general of the Propaganda Department, deputy director of the Political Research Department, and deputy chief editor of the *Red Flag*(红旗) journal, all of the Central Committee of the CCP.

Hu Sheng was persecuted during the "cultural revolution," dismissed from his posts and deprived of work. He later became deputy director of the Party Literature Research Center and director of the Party History Research Center, both of the Central Committee of the CCP. In 1985, he was appointed President of the Chinese Academy of Social Sciences. He was a member of the Standing Committee of the Fourth and Fifth National People's Congresses (1975-83); a member of the Twelfth Central Committee of the CCP (1982-87); and since 1988 has been a vice chairman of the National

Committee of the Chinese People's Consultative Conference.

Hu Sheng was a member of the presidium of the Society of Chinese History and was, for a long time, presidents of the Society of Chinese Communist Party History and the Sun Yat-sen Society.

Hu Sheng devoted himself at an early age, to studying Marxism and to researching and writing on philosophy, history and cultural thought. During China's Anti-Japanese War and Liberation War years, as well as after the founding of the People's Republic of China, he published many essays, theses and articles in various newspapers and journals. He also published books on philosophy and history. A number of essays he published during the new era of socialist modernization which began with the convocation of the Third Plenary Session of the Eleventh Central Committee of the CCP (1978) and which practices reform and opening to the outside world, caught the attention of various circles and were highly valued. His writings are widely influential socially and among school graduates. They are highly appraised by theoreticians and are also of influence abroad. In October of 1990, he was made a member of ACADÉMIE EUROPÉENNE DES SCIENCES, DES ARTS ET DES LETTRES (EUROPEAN ACADEMY OF ARTS, SCIENCES AND HUMANITIES).

His major works are: *Imperialism and Chinese Politics* (1948), *From the Opium War to the May Fourth Movement* (two volumes, 1981), and *The Seventy Years of the Chinese Communist Party* (chief editor, 1991). The two-volume *Collected Works of Hu Sheng* includes major essays he wrote from 1935 through 1948 and from 1979 through 1995. *Imperialism and Chinese Politics*

# Marxism and the Reality
## of China

Over six decades ago, Marxism spread to China and rapidly integrated itself with the workers' movement and other revolutionary movements. Armed with Marxism, the Communist Party of China displayed, even in its infancy, a vitality unprecedented in China's ideological and political arenas.

At the time the Chinese bourgeois revolutionary movement for a bourgeois republic was at an impasse, with slim chances for success, Marxism and the Russian October Revolution broadened horizons for the Chinese people. They, especially the advanced elements among them, gradually came to the conclusion that the future of the Chinese nation, like that of oppressed people throughout the world, lay in socialism and communism.

The earliest Marxists in China believed that the country's problems could be solved simply by copying socialist revolution methods adopted by the Western proletariat. But before long, they came to see from their own experience that this would get them nowhere.

In the giant Asian country of China, then already reduced to a semi-colonial and semi-feudal state, the target of the revolution was not the ordinary bourgeoisie, but imperialism, feudalism, and the comprador-bureaucrat bourgeoisie who ganged up with them. Moreover, the country's political and economic development was uneven and its capitalism underdeveloped. While the ranks of the proletariat were not large, the peasantry had inexhaustible strength that could be called into action.

Apart from the urban petty bourgeoisie which could be its ally, the proletariat could also find allies in other classes and social strata, particularly in the struggle against imperialism. Under these social and historical conditions, China had to take a unique road in developing the revolutionary movement until it entered the stage of socialism.

The Marxists in China once had to oppose such a point of view, i. e. , there had been no class or class struggle in China since ancient times, and modern social development in China could not be interpreted from the viewpoint of class struggle. The reality in China was so "special" that Marxist historical materialism, the theory of class struggle and socialism, were completely impractical in China. Chinese Marxists, investigating into China's history and reality, proved that none of these theories were tenable.

However, China's history has its own characteristics which should be examined when one studies Chinese history through Marxist viewpoint and method.

To cast off the yoke of semi-colonialism and semifeudalism, Marxists in China should use experiences of their own, truly understand reality of China, and apply independently the universal truth of Marxism so as to find a revolutionary road suited to China's reality.

The reality of a country is always subject to change. Revolution means to transform an old world into a new one. However, it is impossible to achieve such a transformation if people merely imagined a proposal for a new world without foundation. The transformation should be conducted in keeping with the objective laws of development and starting from the actual situation of the old world.

This is the distinction between Marxist scientific socialism and Utopian socialism. Of course, it is the same for the reality of a country. Only when people proceeded from the reality of their country could backwardness be transformed.

Generally speaking, Marxists in every country should consider the realities of their own country in applying the common principle. This is particularly important for China.

The history of Marxism's development in China is one of combining the universal truth of Marxism with the concrete practice of the Chinese revolution. Only when the combination was correctly handled did Marxism take root in China, direct the Chinese revolutionary cause and refute thoroughly those who thought Marxism did not fit the reality of China. If not combined with the actuality of China, Marxism would only lead to erroneous principles for the Chinese revolution.

In 1930, Mao Zedong warned against "book worship"（本本主义）, the first time our Party conscientiously and firmly opposed dogmatic tendencies in regard to Marxism. "Book worship" means to lose contact with China's reality, thoughtlessly impose some Marxist conclusions and copy certain foreign patterns or formulas. In essence, it is dogmatism. Mao Zedong said, "The victory of the Chinese revolutionary struggle will rely on Chinese comrades who are familiar with China's situation. " [1]

Marxist theory is neither dogmatic nor unchangeable; it is a guide to action. This is the viewpoint emphasized time and again by Karl Marx and Frederick Engels. The young Marx once said, "The correct theory must be made clear and developed within the concrete conditions and on the basis of the existing state of things. " [2]Mao Zedong's admonition to oppose book worship conformed to the basic spirit of Marxism.

Because China was a semi-colonial, semi-feudal country, its revolution had to proceed in two steps: first achieving victory in the democratic revolution and then starting the socialist revolution.

China's special conditions determined among other things that the proletariat should, and could, win leadership over the democratic revolution; that the proletariat-led democratic revolution should take armed struggle as the major form supplemented with other forms of struggle; that the proletariat must establish rural revolutionary base areas, develop the peasant revolutionary war under its leadership and encircle the cities from the rural areas, and that the proletariat could form a united front with the bourgeoisie under certain conditions.

The Chinese Communists went through countless difficulties (including setbacks and failures) before completely mastering the law governing the development of the Chinese revolution. In the early 1930s, "Left" adventurism (左倾冒险主义)landed the Chinese revolution in a predicament by failing to understand the characteris-

---

[1] Mao Zedong, *Works on Rural Surveys* (in Chinese), Beijing, Renmin Press, 1982, p. 7.

[2] Karl Marx and Frederick Engels, *Collected Works*, New York, International Publishers, 1976, Vol. I, p. 392.

tics of China's semi-colonial and semi-feudal society, the specific status of various social classes in China and particularly the fact that China's bourgeoisie consisted of national bourgeoisie and comprador bourgeoisie, and the characteristics of a revolutionary war led by the proletariat with peasants as its mainstay. They did not apply Marxism to China's specific situation in guiding the Chinese revolution, but copied "formulas" from books.

Although some of the formulas may have been of universal significance, they became utterly useless when separated from concrete practice. And some of these "formulas" were derived from foreign experiences and did not fit in with China's conditions.

In the 1930s the Chinese Communists represented by Mao Zedong swept away these errors of "Left" dogmatism both in theory and practice. Mao Zedong said,

> Our dogmatists are lazy-bones. They refuse to undertake any painstaking study of concrete things; they regard general truths as emerging out of the void and turn them into purely abstract unfathomable formulas.

> The dogmatists... do not understand that conditions differ in different kinds of revolution and so do not understand that different methods should be used to resolve different contradictions; on the contrary, they invariably adopt what they imagine to be an unalterable formula and arbitrarily apply it everywhere, which only causes setbacks to the revolution or makes a sorry mess of what was originally

*well done.* [1]

The victory of the new democratic revolution in 1949 fully proves that the revolutionary road taken by the Chinese people led by the Chinese Communist Party is correct. This road is in keeping with the reality of China and is a Marxist road with Chinese characteristics.

The fact that China realized its transition from new democracy to socialism in a short time after the victory in 1949 is another eloquent proof of the great strength created by integrating Marxist universal truth with China's concrete practice. Although China's semi-colonial and semi-feudal society ended with the victory in 1949, steps in socialist transformation from private ownership of means of production fully considered the features surviving the semi-colonial and semi-feudal society. Therefore, the socialist transformation as a whole was conducted smoothly.

Then, after the basic completion of socialist transformation from private ownership of means of production, namely the basic establishment of the socialist system, did the road of social development in China still retain characteristics of its own? In addition to other elements, did its characteristics still reflect the reality that China was once a semi-colonial and semi-feudal society? These questions are of vital importance to the success or failure of socialism in China.

Marx and Engels scientifically proved that capitalist society would certainly collapse and would be replaced

---

[1] Mao Zedong, *Selected Works*, Beijing, Foreign Languages Press, 1975, Vol. I, pp. 321—322.

by socialist society because of the contradictions it could not solve on its own. The historical mission of the proletariat is to win ruling power through revolution and to replace capitalist private ownership by socialist public ownership so as to accomplish elimination of all classes and create a non-class society.

Marx and Engels once estimated that proletarian revolution would succeed in advanced capitalist countries and would succeed in several countries at the same time. They briefly described measures the proletariat would adopt after they took power in "the most advanced countries," holding that "these measures will of course be different in different countries."[1]

However, both Marx and Engels had cautious attitudes towards the specific future structures and development progression of society. They only made a few comments on principles.

For instance, Engels remarked in 1890 on a discussion in a German publication of product distribution in the future society:

> *Strangely enough it has not struck anyone that, after all, the method of distribution essentially depends on how much there is to distribute, and that this must surely change with the progress of production and social organization, so that the method of distribution may also change presumably. But to everyone who took part in the discussion, "socialist society" appeared not as something undergoing continuous change and progress but as a stable affair*

---

[1]   Karl Marx and Frederick Engels, *Collected Works*, Moscow, Progress Publishers, 1976, Vol. IV, p. 505.

> *fixed once for all, which must, therefore, have a method of distribution fixed once for all. All one can reasonably do, however, is* 1) *to try and discover the method of distribution to be used at the beginning, and* 2) *to try and find the general tendency along which the further development will proceed.* [1]

No doubt, Karl Marx talked in 1875 in detail about the principle of distribution in socialist society in his article, *Critique of the Gotha Programme* . However, his argument was not beyond the scope of what Engels called "reasonable debate."Further, his discussion was directed at phrases by Ferdinand Lassalle: "fair distribution of labour earnings" and "the proceeds of labor belong undiminished with equal right to all members of society. "

In refuting these empty words, Marx pointed out that in a socialist society, distribution of the means of consumption must be tied to the principle of exchange of equal amounts of labor, namely, "a given amount of labor in one form is exchanged for an equal amount of labor in another form. "

Hence, *equal right* here is still — in principle — a bourgeois right. This equal right is an unequal right for different laborers.

But "these defects are inevitable in the first phase of communist society". What we may learn from these statements is that consideration of problems cannot simply proceed from an abstract concept of equality and fair-

---

[1] Karl Marx and Frederick Engels, *Selected Works*, two volumes, Vol. II, pp. 441—442

ness. In fact, it is impossible for Karl Marx to explain in detail methods of distribution in a future society, just as we could not work out a plan directly from Marx's expositions and ignore our social historical conditions as we entered the period of socialist society. Marx was certainly not calling on us to set about abolishing the "defects" immediately.

What Marx stressed was that one could not proceed from the abstract principle of "fairness". If someone thought that existence of unfairness required restrictions in order to achieve fairness, the thinking is not Marxist but a return to the view of Lassalle.

In a word, Marx and Engels in their lifetime could only conceive the basic principles of a socialist society and the general directions it would possibly take.

It is the same for distribution and other questions. Concrete laws governing the development of socialist society in different countries remain to be practiced and studied by later generations.

After the October Revolution, the Bolsheviks led by Lenin once attempted "to introduce the socialist principles of production and distribution by direct assault, i. e. , in the shortest, quickest and most direct way". [1] But they failed. Therefore, they had to change their minds and adopt methods conforming to the historical characteristics of the Russian society.

Lenin once thought that all nations would enter the socialist society. However, their ways were not entirely the same and each had characteristics of its own. He considered that possibilities existed for colonial and

[1]   V. I. Lenin, *Collected Works*, Moscow, Progress Publishers, Vol. 33, p. 93

backward countries to avoid development of the capitalist stage and transit directly to the socialist society by
going through a certain revolution.

He held that differences among various nations and
countries would remain for a long, long period of time
even after the realization of the dictatorship of the proletariat all over the world. So, each should apply

> *the fundamental principles of communism (Soviet
> power and the dictatorship of the proletariat), cor-
> rectly modify these principles in certain particulars,
> correctly adapt and apply them to national and na-
> tional-state distinctions.* [1]

These declarations by Lenin merit attention. All
nations and countries will certainly become socialist societies. However, the "Great Harmony of the World" (世
界大同)is in the distant future. These countries will not
only arrive at socialism by various means but will also
develop it differently according to their own conditions.

There still exists the problem of integrating the universal truth of Marxism with concrete practices of different countries during socialist construction. China,
which has gone through a special road from semi-colonial and semi-feudal society to socialist society, should
pay special attention to this problem.

Human history shows a socialist society does not
come out of a void. It is established on the basis of civi-
lizations created by humanity through several thousand
years, particularly the civilization created by capitalism,
which is much more advanced than any previous ones.

---

[1]  *Ibid*. ,Vol. 31.

Capitalism created tremendous productive forces and, in conjunction with these forces, developed full-fledged education, culture, science and technology, economic management and so on.

All these furnish the "building blocks" needed for socialism once the political power of a developed capitalist country falls into the hands of the proletariat and the socialist public ownership of the means of production is established.

However, China is totally different. Its socialist society grew out of semi-colonialism and semi-feudalism where elements of capitalism existed but were underdeveloped. It has never experienced the stage of developed capitalism, and the "legacy" it inherited from the old society contained virtually nothing of what a capitalist society could have offered.

For that reason, in building socialism China will inevitably encounter many special problems and difficulties in the economic, cultural and political arenas. We should therefore conscientiously solve these problems within the framework of the socialist system and learn everything necessary for socialism, which other nations have learned under the capitalist system. Just as the democratic revolution had to be carried out in the light of China's reality — a semi-colonial and semi-feudal society, in travelling our own socialist road, we should again take this reality into consideration.

Perhaps some people would say that since China has many special problems and difficulties in building its socialism, why does it not build capitalism first and then socialism?

This question merits answering. If the proletariat had not led the new democratic revolution to victory,

China would have remained a semi-colonial and semi-feudal society or even been reduced to the colony of a single imperialist country.

China's social and historical conditions, international circumstances included, did not and could not make China an independent capitalist country. From an historical materialist view, we must note that China had not been in a position to take this road even if development from capitalism to socialism were a "shortcut"; and it is by no means a shortcut anyway.

Developing capitalism means a long and painful road for the working people. Now that the proletariat and the working people have won the socialist victory directly through democratic revolution within a special historical condition, why should they choose the long and painful way out of fear of problems and difficulties in building socialism?

China could not develop capitalism from its feudal society. In modern times it became a backward country trampled by the imperialist countries. This is a misfortune of history.

However, the Chinese people, guided by Marxism, have embarked on the socialist road after experiencing the semi-colonial and semi-feudal society for more than one hundred years. This new route is a good fortune for history even though there will inevitably be many special difficulties along the road.

Absence of the stage of full-grown capitalism in our history has caused some special difficulties but there are also some advantages to it. Tempered by long years of national suffering and revolutionary struggles, the Chinese people have generated an outstanding tradition of unity and hard struggle under the banner of patriotism.

Our working class has rarely been influenced by social reformism, and the "labor aristocracy" which appeared in capitalist countries has never appeared in our country. In the long years of revolutionary wars, land reform and the cooperative movement, our peasants established a close alliance with the working class and had great confidence in the leadership of the Communist Party.

Our intellectuals from the old society are, generally speaking, imbued with strong patriotism although they received bourgeois education. Their experiences in the old and new societies have convinced them that only the socialist system can make China prosperous and powerful. After the socialist transformation from private ownership of the means of production was undertaken by the peaceful "buying out" policy, the majority of the Chinese bourgeoisie consciously remolded themselves into laborers earning their own livings and were willing to contribute their experiences and abilities to the socialist motherland.

Similar changes took place among other members of the upper-strata of the old society. These phenomena provide favorable conditions for building socialism. Fully utilizing these conditions will, of course, help overcome our weaknesses; but if we pay no attention to overcoming our weaknesses, we will not be able to fully tap our strengths.

Generally speaking, building socialism is an arduous task. Since entering socialism, China has had to face problems which developed capitalist countries will not encounter when they become socialist societies (these countries, in turn, will have problems we do not have). What are our special problems? For example, socialized production in our society as a whole, especially in the vast countryside, remains at a very low level and the commodity economy is underdeveloped; there is still much illiteracy, education is not yet universal and our educational facilities are scanty; our science and technology are backward and we have few intellectuals and even fewer highly qualified intellectuals, and we lack experience in running large-scale industrial and commercial enterprises.

In politics, China has never had a bourgeois democratic system. Bourgeois democracy and legal systems are based on exploitation of labor by capital, a deceit imposed on the masses of working people. However, Marxists, while exposing the nature of bourgeois democratic systems, always point out that their replacement of a feudal system is a significant progress in human history. Of course, socialism could not inherit the legacy of a political system as it would the legacy of large-scale production and cultural and educational facilities from the capitalist society (these legacies can be utilized by socialism as soon as they are annexed).

However, a nation's experiences of bourgeois democracy and the bourgeois legal system affect its socialist democracy. China has no such experiences, it has only a democratic tradition which is no doubt valuable, built up within revolutionary armies and in revolutionary base areas during the protracted revolutionary wars. But, for the society as a whole, we must inaugurate socialist democracy and legal system by eliminating the remnants of the feudal system's superstructure.

After the basic completion of the socialist transformation from private ownership of the means of production, the Eighth National Congress of the Communist

Party of China pointed out in August 1956 that the major task of the Chinese people in the future was to develop the productive forces and realize national industrialization so as to meet the increasing material and cultural needs of the people.

This principle was based on the fact that after the establishment of the socialist system social productive forces were still very backward. Some capitalist countries (not the most advanced ones) perhaps were more backward than others in social productive forces when they changed into socialist societies. However, China's social productive forces were backward not only in comparison with those of the foreign countries. To consolidate and expand the socialist system which has already been set up, the existing social productive forces are badly insufficient. This is a condition created by China's special historical background.

Generally speaking, it is impossible for the socialist system to be complete and perfect at the very beginning, especially when its social productive forces are backward. Therefore, while developing its social productive forces China should also continuously perfect its socialist relations of production and superstructure to fit its reality. Although the Eighth National Congress of the Party did not clarify all questions completely, it is correct for the Congress to make development of social productive forces its major task.

The socialist system has indeed brought unprecedented growth to China's social productive forces. In summing up the achievements of the thirty-two years since the founding of the People's Republic, the *Resolution on Certain Questions in the History of Our Party Since the Founding of the People's Republic of China*, adopted by the Party Central Committee in June 1981, points out that *"we have scored signal successes in industrial construction and have gradually set up an independent and fairly comprehensive industrial base and economic system"*.

*"Conditions prevailing in agricultural production have experienced a remarkable change, giving rise to big increases in production."*

*"There has been a substantial growth in urban and rural commerce and in foreign trade."*

*"Considerable progress has been made in education, science, culture, public health and physical culture."*

All these point to the fact that the economic and cultural situation in China today is very much changed from what it was in early post-liberation days or when the socialist transformation had just been completed. Although our socialist construction has traversed a tortuous road and suffered many setbacks due to "Left" mistakes, the achievements are undeniable.

The "Left" mistakes committed by the Party in socialist construction culminated in the launching of the "cultural revolution" (1966—1976) which continued for a long time and affected the overall situation.

These, of course, were due to the complex social and historical factors which were profoundly analyzed and expounded in the *Resolution on Certain Questions in the History of Our Party Since the Founding of the People's Republic of China*. One of the major lessons we must draw from our "Left" mistakes is that if one turns a blind eye to China's actual conditions and becomes dogmatic about certain "formulas" (which, more often than not, are derived from one-sided interpretation of Marxism), then one cannot correctly guide the revolution and socialist construction.

Since China had not gone through the stage of developed capitalism, we are inevitably confronted with problems to be solved, many new things we have to learn and a good deal of complicated work to accomplish after we entered socialism. It will take us a long period of time. We will commit gross errors if we fail to take note of this and expect to quickly fulfil the tasks of the socialist period and move on to communism, or if we believe that every problem can be solved by one or two mass movements.

The contradiction between the production relations and the productive forces and the contradiction between superstructure and the economic base still exist in a socialist society. Bearing this in mind is of great significance to our probes into the laws of the development of socialist society. But this is, after all, one of the general laws.

If we fail to proceed from China's actual conditions, we will never pinpoint what needs to be reformed in the superstructure or the relations of production. If we undertake a "reform" according to such abstract concepts as "the bigger the size, the higher the level of public ownership, the better," then inevitably we will see more practices like "everyone eating from the same big rice pot," which hinder the development of productive forces.

The formula of "a revolution in which one class overthrows the other" only applies to societies with class exploitation; using it in a socialist society which has abolished the system of exploitation of man by man can only bring harm to the socialist superstructure and the relations of production.

"Socialism should fight the bourgeoisie" was regarded as the soul of the so-called "continuing the revolution under the dictatorship of the proletariat". This formula neither distinguishes the period of transition to socialism from the period in which the socialist system has already been established, nor makes a specific analysis of things that could seemingly be labelled bourgeois. It even slaps this label on people right and left, and we have all seen the disastrous results of abusing this label.

It goes without saying that during the socialist period it is necessary to combat decadent bourgeois ideas and crack down on any bourgeois force that seeks to undermine socialism. However, in our socialist endeavors we should learn all useful things produced under the capitalist system. Some of these (such as natural sciences and technology) have no class nature.

Some (such as the management system for large-scale production) bear class hallmarks but should still be carefully distinguished and analyzed so we can absorb and remold them; this is of special significance under China's historical conditions.

In a capitalist society commodity production grows at a rate higher than in any previous societies, but according to an assumption by Marx and Engels, it will be liquidated in future societies.

In China, however, commodity production, rather than being fully developed, remains weak and small. If we equate commodity production with capitalism, regardless of China's reality, and if we regard the assumptions of the creators of Marxism as a formula that can be applied arbitrarily, then development of our socialist production will be impeded.

The slogan "Down with bourgeois reactionary academic authorities" is a slogan with no traces of Marxism. What it has eliminated is not authorities of "bourgeoisie," just as, under the label of "persons in power within the Party taking the capitalist road," the "capitalist-roaders" are not bourgeoisie at all.

Suppose there are indeed academic authorities who persevere in a bourgeois world outlook, what attitude should the proletariat take to them? No doubt, the correct one is to help them remold themselves by proper methods and at the same time, learn conscientiously from them in order to take over their scholarship, or critically assimilate their knowledge.

Since they are authorities, why don't we learn from them? Bourgeois reactionary power can be overthrown through revolutionary mass movement, but under no circumstances should, or can "academic authorities" be suppressed by the same method.

Taking into consideration that intellectuals in China are not numerous but very few, and that there is a shortage of academic authorities, this slogan is absolutely ridiculous.

Public ownership of the means of production, the principle of distribution "to each according to his or her work" as well as planned and proportionate development of the national economy represent only the general laws of the socialist system.

If we rely solely on these general laws but fail to integrate them with our concrete conditions, we will accomplish nothing. If we design a "pure" and "perfect" socialism according to these laws and become obsessed with abstract concept of "perfection", we can get nothing but guiding principles estranged from reality and spoil what could have been done well.

During the "cultural revolution", China's situation was wrongly assessed and it was believed that bourgeois reactionary forces were ubiquitous and, worse still, the wrong conclusion was made that the status quo could be changed and a "purest" and "most perfect" socialist society established with one or two thrusts of the mass struggle. All these, needless to say, are Utopian ideas which bring nothing good, but do great harm.

Marx once mentioned in a letter in 1877 that the Party of Germany was influenced by some people

> who want to give socialism a 'superior, idealistic' orientation, that is to say, to replace its materialistic basis (which demands serious objective study from anyone who tries to use it) by modern mythology with its goddesses of Justice, Liberty, Equality, and Fraternity.

Therefore, Marx said with emotion:

> Utopian socialism which for decades we have been clearing out of the German workers' heads with so much effort and labor — and it is their freedom from it which has made them theoretically (and therefore also practically) superior to the French and English — utopian socialism, playing with fantastic pictures of the future structure of society, is again rampant.... [1]

The "Leftists" we mention here also enshrine and worship some "goddesses." Although they are opposite to the bourgeois goddesses of liberty, equality and fraternity, these socialist "goddesses" who are "most revo-

---

[1]   Karl Marx and Frederick Engels, *Selected Correspondence.*

lutionary," "most pure" and "most fair," also cause socialism to forfeit its essential materialistic base.

Mao Zedong made monumental achievements in his decades-long efforts to base the Chinese revolution theoretically on materialism. Mao Zedong Thought applies universal Marxist principles to China's concrete historical conditions and sums up the creative experiences of the practice of the Chinese revolution.

It is the crystallization of the Chinese-Communists' collective wisdom, but Mao Zedong played an exceptionally important role in its formation. Long periods of practice showed that he was a great Marxist ready at any time to break new ground.

In his later years, however, he depended too heavily on practical experiences gained during the protracted revolutionary struggle while paying inadequate attention to conscientiously studying the new situation and new problems arising after China had entered the socialist period.

As a result, he gradually departed from the principle of integrating theory with practice, which he had always advocated. While he believed he was blazing a new trail for socialism, he was actually bound hand and foot by a number of abstract concepts and formulas which were divorced from reality. This serves as a profound lesson for future generations.

To correct the "Left" mistakes and lead China's socialist construction onto a correct road, it is necessary to restore the tradition of Mao Zedong Thought, i. e. , the tradition of combining universal Marxist principles with the concrete practice of the Chinese revolution. It is necessary to resolutely safeguard the materialist foundation of socialism and at the same time dare to creatively use

Marxism to solve China's problems.

This was precisely what the Communist Party of China did at its Third Plenary Session of the Eleventh Party Central Committee held in December 1978. Since then, the Party has, in its guidelines, gradually accomplished the arduous task of correcting past wrongs in all fields of endeavor; the Party and state principles and policies have scored remarkable achievements, bringing about an unprecedentedly excellent situation in the economic, political and cultural fields.

The Party and the state have resolutely shifted emphasis of their work to socialist economic construction, which is not merely a return to the principles and policies laid down at the Eighth Party Congress in 1956. Our experiences over the past thirty-odd years have brought home to us that in socialist revolution and construction, we should, rather than being dogmatic about what is called universal formulas, use the Marxist stand, viewpoint and method to understand the reality of China and we should formulate our principles, policies and measures on this basis.

Of course, it is necessary to refer to the experiences of other countries, but on no account should we simply pattern ourselves after them. Both in understanding and practice of socialist construction, our Party has become far more mature than at any time since the founding of the People's Republic.

China's current conditions are vastly different from what they were in 1956, the year the socialist system was established. The socialist system has endured severe tests over these three decades and has driven a solid root into the vast territory of China.

Our socialist construction has been crowned with

tremendous successes, and the mental outlooks of workers, peasants and intellectuals have undergone enormous
changes. These are China's basic conditions, which we
should bear in mind in all our endeavors. Both the
achievements we have made and the changes that have
taken place in the course of building socialism deserve
our earnest analyses and study, but due attention should
also be paid to our difficulties and weaknesses resulting
from the fact that our socialist society evolved from a semi-colonial, semi-feudal society and that China has not
undergone a period of full-fledged capitalism.

There are other factors that should not be neglected
in studying the concrete conditions of China: the huge
population in sharp contrast to the limited arable land,
opulent natural resources most of which wait to be
tapped, and so on.

In the rural areas, we have adopted various forms
of the responsibility system which bases remunerations
on output and contracts production tasks along special-
ized lines. This has vigorously generated sideline occu-
pations and other diverse economic undertakings and has
expanded commodity production and exchange. In economic fields, we have carried out structural reforms centered on improving economic results. And, in particular, we have restructured the management system. We
have made education and science one of our major strategic focuses in developing the economy and are striving to
maximize the role of intellectuals and to train as many
new intellectuals as possible.

We have strengthened socialist democracy and improved the socialist legal system. On the basis of self-re-
liance, we have developed economic cooperation and
technical exchanges with foreign countries.

All these and other efforts are conducive to developing the current socialist system and achievements in socialist construction; they also help us to overcome weaknesses that resulted from the absence of the stage of capitalism in Chinese history.

We can certainly overcome the special difficulties caused by social and historical conditions, and build socialism in a distinctive Chinese way provided we comprehensively study and understand our nation's specific conditions and, in the light of these conditions, apply universal Marxist principles to the construction of socialist material and spiritual civilization in our country.

China is still backward compared with developed capitalist countries, although considerable progress has been made in its economy and culture over the past thirty-odd years after it moved out of the semi-colonial and semi-feudal society.

As for this, shall we feel discouraged, or think that socialism and Marxism are ineffective in China? Of course, we should not. Some people lose their heads because they don't understand that historical conditions require that China must, under its socialist system, fulfil the development course of economy and culture which has been completed by other countries under capitalist system.

Thirty years is but a short period in history. Western capitalist countries have gone through two to three hundred years to reach modernization at present-day levels.

Depending on the integration of Marxism with concrete practice of China and the socialist system, China can not only travel such a course without the exploitation of the working people, but can also complete the course in a fairly short time. This is what we are striving to do and we will do it well as long as we try our best.

Since the Third Plenary Session of the Eleventh Party Central Committee, we have scientifically summed up both positive and negative experiences, and have blazed a trail to the building of socialism with Chinese characteristics. Now, we are struggling to create a new situation in all fields of socialist modernization according to the program formulated by the Twelfth National Congress of the Communist Party.

Of course, this should be enriched and perfected through practice. During the democratic revolution, we opened up according to China's specific historical conditions a Marxist road with our own characteristics, resulting in a new development of Marxism. Just as we did in the past, we will break a new trail of Marxism in a distinctive Chinese way to build socialism.

(First published in *Red Flag*, no. 6, 16 March, 1983).

# Capitalism Is Impractical
# in China

China's embarkation on the socialist road is an objective fact. However, some people maintain or advocate that the socialist system is undesirable in China and that China should have adopted the capitalist system. So, a serious discussion should be conducted on this erroneous view.

Why must China only take the socialist road? Or, in other words, why is capitalism impractical in China?

If merely citing facts to show that socialism is more advanced than capitalism, the answer is both incomplete and unscientific. When capitalism first emerged in Western Europe, some advanced thinkers opposed it, believing that only socialist and communist systems conform to reason. Their good intentions could not determine the course of the societal development there because the capitalist system continued to develop in West European countries.

Marxist theory of scientific socialism has proved that capitalism is bound to fail because of its inherent contradictions, and socialism will inevitable rise in its stead. In developing social production, bringing benefits to humanity, and creating conditions for the free development of all people, the socialist system can demonstrate its incomparable superiority over the capitalist system.

However, in answering the question of why China must take the socialist road, one cannot just rely on an abstract and general comparison between socialism and capitalism. We must look at the history of Chinese society.

# I

Historically, China went through a prolonged period of feudalism for about 3,000 years. Between the 1840s and 1850s, Western countries launched two Opium Wars and the invasion of China which followed the wars prompted the Taiping Heavenly Kingdom (太平天国) peasant revolution (1851—1864), resulting in unprecedented changes in China's society. That is when China's modern history began.

Many patriots tried to practice capitalism as a way of expediting China's progress and eliminating its poverty and vulnerability to attack. Although capitalism exploits the working people, its replacement of feudalism is progress, and generally speaking it can lead a country to prosperity. However, capitalism is impractical under modern Chinese conditions.

Modern machine industry and steamships first appeared in China in the 1850s. However, they were operated with foreign capital and limited in number at first. It was not until the end of the nineteenth century when their numbers increased. Military industries controlled by feudal bureaucrats appeared in China in the 1860s.

It is noteworthy that, during the 1860s and 1870s, private Chinese capitalist enterprises did begin to emerge. This shows that an embryonic potential for the capitalist mode of production existed in the feudal society. But it grew through difficulties in modern China and had never developed into an independent and powerful force.

In the vast rural areas, feudal land-based relationships occupied a dominant position. All the previous regimes, without exception, used the feudal landlord class as their major power base (or one of the major power bases), and tried hard to preserve the feudal land-based relationship. Although capitalism existed in Chinese society, it was feudalism that dominated, hence the term "semi-feudal society".

Why, in China, did the new-born capitalist economy and the political force representing the capitalist economy fail to prevail over feudalism? In the seventeenth and eighteenth centuries, these newborn forces conquered difficulties and setbacks and finally prevailed in European countries. Modern China, however, endured a special set of historical circumstances. Namely, China, under imperialist invasion, became a semi-colonial country.

Through the end of the nineteenth century and at the beginning of the twentieth century, the world's land mass had been almost carved up by a few imperialist countries — Britain, Tsarist Russia and other European countries, as well as the United States in North America and the budding Japan in the East. They forced nearly all regions with backward economies in the world to be their colonies.

Thus, the history of "opening up" created by Western colonialists, starting from the sixteenth century, was a story of blood and tears. Colonialists barbarously plundered and exploited all backward tribes and nationalities in their paths, even denying them the right to exist by trying to eliminate these tribes and nationalities; on the other hand, colonialist rule was established over nationalities they could not eliminate.

Capitalist aggressors changed the world to suit their objectives. To meet their needs, colonial regimes imposed new mode of production on these countries and regions. Also, for the same purposes, various kinds of precapitalist relationships were preserved and maintained.

In colonies, the contrast between the paradise of the rich and the hell of the poor was especially sharp. Except for the "prosperity" and "civilization" of a few cities and regions where colonialists lived, vast areas were enveloped in poverty and darkness, and people were heavily exploited and suppressed. That is why many colonial countries were underdeveloped when they achieved independence after World War II.

The imperialist powers forced Chinese rulers to yield to their gunboat diplomacy, and their political and economic forces penetrated the country. They forcibly occupied a number of China's coastal ports, established "concessions" in many Chinese cities and racked their brains to find ways of carving up China.

However, they could not reduce China completely to a colony for two reasons: First, there was great potential in the Chinese people for resistance to foreign aggression. Though this potential erupted in infantile and spontaneous forms early on, it perplexed the aggressors who began to see that it was difficult to rule over hundreds of millions of Chinese people directly. Second, either an occupation of China by one country alone or partition of China by a few countries would inevitably lead to intense conflicts between these powers. To avoid this, the imperialists let China maintain its *status quo* while they carved out spheres of influence according to their own strength, shared the benefits and jointly decided China's destiny.

China remained an independent country in form, but, in essence, it had lost its integrity and sovereignty. China became a semi-colony plundered by almost all the imperialist countries in the world, large and small. During the 1930s, Japanese imperialists tried to swallow China by force, but ended up in complete defeat. This was the first such defeat in the history of imperialist invasions of China.

The very purpose of foreign imperialists in monopolizing China's foreign trade and in opening factories, mines, shipping companies and banks in China was not to make China a capitalist country. On the contrary, they excluded and oppressed the Chinese.

This was the main cause for underdevelopment of China's national capitalism. During World War I (1914 —18), all the imperialist countries, except Japan, were busy with the European war and had no time to attend to the East. During that time, and for one or two years thereafter, China's national industry and commerce flourished, and the period was called the "golden time". But the imperialist countries reasserted themselves after the war and the "golden time" ended quickly.

This proved further that without national independence, China's capitalism could not develop freely. Of course, when China lost its independence and sovereignty, development of foreign trade and utilization of foreign capital to serve China's interests and needs were out of the question.

These imperialist powers created a comprador class

of Chinese in their service, and tried their utmost to maintain the feudal land-based relationship and its corresponding social framework in China. Warlords, bureaucrats and political parties, all with compradors and feudal landlords as their power bases, were chosen agents of the imperialists in dominating China.

The imperialists supported their agents militarily and financially, and through them, bled the Chinese people white. When any of these agents collapsed, the imperialists replaced them with others. Although the feudal forces were corrupt and backward, they, supported by imperialists and colluding with compradors, became powerful bastions.

At the root of modern China's poverty and backwardness and its inability to develop from the feudal system towards capitalism is imperialist aggression and oppression.

## II

To eliminate poverty and backwardness and to make progress, China needed to be free of imperialist oppression and to become an independent country. Abolishing feudalism presupposed throwing off imperialism. And they together defined the basic tasks of China's democratic revolution. Who could accomplish these tasks? Had there been a bourgeois force able to carry this off, China would have developed capitalism independently.

Reformists headed by Kang Youwei （康 有 为，1858—1927） were the earliest political activists with bourgeois features in modern China. They were deeply affected by the suffering under imperialist aggression and oppression and were strongly patriotic. They pro-

posed capitalist programs in political and economic
fields, trying to carry them out through the emperor and
the existing institutions,but they soon failed.

The Tong Meng Hui（同盟会,China Revolutionary
League）, established in 1905 and headed by Sun Yat-sen
（孙中山,1866—1925）, advanced a complete revolutionary program making a bourgeois democratic republic as
its goal, and struggled to carry out this program.

Sun, who had noticed shortcomings of capitalism in
Western countries and who was influenced by the socialist movement which was growing in the West, tried to
develop some socialist traits in his program. But, at
root, Sun and his comrades were seeking to develop capitalism in China.

The China Revolutionary League led the 1911 Revolution which overthrew the Qing Dynasty（1644 —
1911）. This feudal monarchy which had long been a tool
of imperialism was replaced by the Republic of China
（1912—49）. So, it was a victory.

But this did not weaken the hold of imperialist
forces in China. The fruits of revolution were wrested
away by imperialist follower Yuan Shikai（袁世凯,1859
—1916）and other Northern Warlords. China was still a
semi-colonial and semi-feudal country, remaining poor
and backward. The 1911 Revolution did not achieve its
intended aim.

After this revolution, however, numerous political
groups emerged. Many of them were composed of politi-
cians and bureaucrats and they faded as fast as they appeared. Some petty bourgeois political groupings which
declared themselves anarchist or socialist were short-
lived because they were divorced from reality and the
masses.

However，the Kuomintang（国民党），which grew out of the China Revolutionary League and the Progressive Party（进步党），with Liang Qichao（梁启超，1873—1929）as its spiritual leader，did exert some political influence in the early years of the republic. Liang, who took part in the Reform Movement of 1898, and his fellow progressives were for the development of capitalism in China, but did not oppose imperialism or feudalism. On the contrary, they relied on feudal warlords, so eventually they became only a small part of the official circle, capricious in their views and pursuing fame and gain.

The Kuomintang in the early years of the republic absorbed many bureaucrats and opportunists and lost the revolutionary nature of the China Revolutionary League. Under pressure from Yuan Shikai, the Kuomintang split. Sun Yat-sen and a few fellow Kuomintang members founded the Chinese Revolutionary Party which was too small to lead the struggle against Yuan Shikai.

After Yuan died, Sun Yat-sen dissolved the Chinese Revolutionary Party to reestablish the Kuomintang in october 1919. Although it claimed a large membership, its members came from diverse backgrounds and discipline was lax. Before 1924, the party was paralyzed and could offer no political proposals capable of mobilizing the people. Based on its success in the 1911 Revolution, its nucleus—Sun Yat-sen and a few of his comrades—persisted in working for progress and against Northern Warlords, and the Kuomintang, after suffering repeated setbacks, established political power in Guangdong Province to oppose the Northern Warlord government. This kept the Kuomintang as the main progressive party in China's political life.

In 1923, Sun Yat-sen decided to accept Russian aid and cooperate with the newly-founded Communist Party of China. He reorganized the Kuomintang and revitalized it. In January 1924, the Kuomintang held its First National Congress with participation of Communist Party members (individual Communists who joined the Kuomintang), the first in the thirteen years after the 1911 Revolution.

Cooperation between the Kuomintang and the Communist Party did not stop when Sun Yat-sen died in March 1925. It is the cooperation between the two parties that made it possible to achieve unification of the revolutionary base areas in Guangdong and Guangxi, the establishment of the National Revolutionary Army, the surge of workers and peasants movements, the launch of the Northern Expedition(北伐) and the establishment of nationwide prestige for the Kuomintang.

If the revolution had continued under Kuomintang-Communist cooperation, what would have happened in China? The programs as declared at the Kuomintang First National Congress were to abolish imperialist privileges in China, overthrow the warlords, and provide peasants with land of their own. Realization of these programs would not have built China into a socialist country but would create favorable conditions for development of national capitalism.

Even though the programs included control of capital, meaning that China would not emulate capitalist countries by allowing the national economy to be monopolized by a few capitalists, they would not at all build China into a socialist country.

The national revolution, centered around Kuo-

mintang-Communist cooperation, was halted halfway after betrayal by the right wing of the Kuomintang. In
1927, the Kuomintang came to power on the strength of
achievements in the national revolution under Kuomintang-Communist cooperation, overthrowing the Northern Warlords regime, but also through massacre of
Communists and other revolutionaries.

Rather than discuss the 22-year Kuomintang rule
here, a single question needs to be addressed: Did the
Kuomintang develop China's national industry, commerce and capitalism?

The answer is negative. A good example is the cotton textile industry in the first ten years (1927—36) under the rule of the Kuomintang, just before outbreak of
the War of Resistance against Japan (1937—45). This
example is used because the textile industry was the
most developed in China, while heavy industry at that
time was underdeveloped (steel output in 1933 was only
35,000 tons).

In 1927, China had 3.7 million spindles and in 1936
the figure was up to 5.1 million. Those owned by foreign concerns increased by nearly 50 percent from 1.6
million to 2.4 million during this period, most owned by
the Japanese and a small proportion by the British. The
proportion of foreign-owned spindles climbed from 42.9
percent to 46.2 percent. Chinese ownership increased
from 2.1 million to 2.7 million, only a 31 percent increase, and the proportional ownership dropped from
57.1 percent to 53.8 percent.

The number of weaving looms rose from 29,788 in
1927 to 58,439 in 1936, with foreign ownership increasing from 16,329 to 32,936 (a 100 percent increase), accounting for 54.8 percent in 1927 and 58.1percent in

1936. Chinese ownership increased from 13,459 to 25,503, an increase of 90 percent, while its proportion of the nation's total dropped from 45.2 percent to 41.9 percent. [1]

The same source asserts: "In 1932, China's cotton textile industry was on the brink of bankruptcy as taxes and levies were exorbitant, the unspun cotton was expensive and the yarn cheap. In the second half of 1935, of the 59 cotton mills run by the Chinese, 24 were closed and 14 had to dismiss workers. It is wrong to take the number of spindles and looms as a criterion for judging the state of the cotton textile industry. "[2]

That is to say, the actual situation was worse than the figures suggest. Under the Kuomintang rule, Chinese national capital in the textile industry was declining while the imperialist capital in China was growing rapidly.

The Kuomintang could not rid China of imperialist rule and make the country independent; to the contrary, its very existence depended on imperialist support. It was also impossible for the Kuomintang to unify China because many groups within the regime struggled for power, causing large-scale civil wars. The Kuomintang could neither carry out Sun Yat-sen's proposal for land to the tiller nor its own plan for a 25 percent reduction in land rent.

So, feudal land relations remained unchanged. The Kuomintang could not change the semi-colonial and semi-feudal condition of China, and certainly could not

---

[1] *Bank Weekly*, the 30th Anniversary Issue, 1948, pp. 335 — 336.

[2] *Ibid.*, p. 255.

build China into a capitalist country. In a word, the
Kuomintang betrayed not only the purpose of the First
National Congress at which the Kuomintang cooperated
with the Communist Party, but also betrayed the Chinese Revolutionary League's heritage.

When the Kuomintang came to power, the middle
bourgeoisie hoped it would develop China's capitalist
economy, but was disappointed and became all the more
disappointed during and after the War of Resistance A-
gainst Japan.

## III

When the Chinese Communist Party was founded in
1921 it was a small group of several dozen people. At
the time they saw socialist revolution as their immediate
task, but soon realized that the revolution for China's
progress would have to start with struggle against imperialism and feudalism.

The Communist Party's active participation in the
national revolution of 1925 to 1927 expanded its ranks to
nearly sixty thousand. The Kuomintang's massacre in
1927 reduced its forces again. But the Chinese Communists, with indomitable spirit, shifted their focus and
mobilized the masses mainly in rural areas, where they
carried out land reform, founded the Red Army, and set
up revolutionary base areas.

On what issue did the Communist Party differentiate itself from the Kuomintang? The difference between
them at the time was not yet about whether China
should practice socialism. Although the ultimate objective of the Communist Party was to realize socialism and
communism, its immediate program at the time was to

eliminate feudal land relations.

Without such land reform, it is impossible for capitalism to grow, to say nothing of socialism. Mao Zedong commented: "Taken in its social setting, the dispute between the two parties is essentially over this issue of agrarian relations."[1]

A fundamental task of China's democratic revolution was to oppose imperialism. When Japanese aggression made national interests increasingly China's primary concern, the Chinese Communist Party proposed an end to the civil war and unity to resist Japanese aggressors. It also changed its policy of confiscating land of the landlords to that of reductions in rent and interest.

This promoted formation of the anti-Japanese national united front which also included Kuomintang rulers who agreed to resist Japanese aggression. Although it experienced numerous twists and turns, the Anti-Japanese War, waged on a second round of cooperation between the Communist Party and the Kuomintang, eventually ended in victory.

Since the Communist Party persisted in fighting against Japanese aggression behind enemy lines, and because it upheld a national united front policy which rallied the majority of the Chinese people, it grew into a big party of more than 1.2 million members by the end of war. The Kuomintang and the Communist Party then became the two major political parties in deciding China's future and destiny.

After the War of Resistance Against Japan, the Kuomintang and the Communist Party (as well as other democratic parties) began a series of negotiations. To

---

[1] Mao Zedong, *On Coalition Government*, 1945.

achieve peace, democracy and progress, the Communist
Party suggested establishing a democratic coalition government. Although the Kuomintang agreed with the
proposal at first, it later reneged and, backed by U. S.
imperialists, launched an all-out civil war.

We may say that it was the Kuomintang's anti-
Communist volte-face in 1927 which led to the failure of
the national revolution and deprived China of a chance to
create conditions for developing capitalism. The Kuomintang rejection of a democratic coalition government
after the end of the anti-Japanese War again lost China
that opportunity.

Mao Zedong said in 1945 in *On Coalition Government*
(论联合政府), "Some people fail to understand why,
far from fearing capitalism, Communists should advocate its development under certain given conditions. Our
answer is simple. The substitution of a certain degree of
capitalist development for the oppression of foreign imperialism and domestic feudalism is not only an advance
but an unavoidable process. It benefits the proletariat as
well as the bourgeoisie, the former perhaps more than
the latter. It is not domestic capitalism but foreign imperialism and domestic feudalism that are superfluous in
China today; indeed, we have too little of capitalism. "

This was the basis on which the Communist Party
at the time was willing to continue to cooperate with the
Kuomintang in building the country after the War of Resistance Against Japan.

What the Communists said about a "certain degree
of capitalist development" did not imply turning China
into a capitalist country. Dr. Sun Yat-sen, the great
forerunner of China's democratic revolution, had pondered the type of state which would emerge after the vic-

tory of democratic revolution in China.

On one hand he proposed to develop capitalism and, on the other hand, he thought China should not follow the beaten track of Western capitalism because he was anxious that it would, in time, lead to a socialist revolution with bloodshed. The Chinese Communists had also thought of this question time and again. In the 1930s they proposed "non-capitalist" development. Since the bourgeoisie could not lead the democratic revolution to completion and the proletariat was playing the leading role in this revolution, it would be impossible for China to establish a state under bourgeois dictatorship after the victory of the revolution.

Nevertheless, "non-capitalism" was an ambiguous concept. In the 1940s, Mao Zedong advanced the concept of new-democratic revolution and a new-democratic republic, a definite answer to this question, proposed in the light of China's specific conditions. Mao Zedong explained that the new-democratic republic was a republic under "a joint dictatorship of all the revolutionary classes".

The country's economy was to be one in which the state "will own the big banks and the big industrial and commercial enterprises". "But the republic will neither confiscate capitalist private property in general nor forbid the development of such capitalist production if it does not 'dominate the livelihood of the people', for China's economy is still very backward". [1] Of course, a new-democratic republic assumes accomplishment of anti-imperialist and anti-feudalistic tasks as its prerequisites.

---

[1] Mao Zedong, *On New Democracy*, 1940.

However, the Kuomintang leaders did not think foreign imperialism was superfluous in China. Instead, they welcomed U. S. imperialists in replacing Japanese imperialists to actually rule over China in the hope of receiving their support, which they certainly did.

Nor did Kuomintang leaders consider feudalism superfluous in China. They refused to replace feudalism with democratic land reform and democratic politics. Instead of creating favorable conditions for the development of national capitalism, the Kuomintang leading clique built an enormous bureaucratic capital over itself.

Emerged prior to the War of Resistance Against Japan, bureaucratic capital proliferated during the war. The bureaucrat-capitalists took the opportunity to monopolize finance, annex private capital, and embezzle financial aid provided by the U. S. government.

After the war, bureaucratic capital swelled to bursting as property of the enemy and puppet personnel in Japanese-occupied areas was appropriated and unscrupulous pillaging of people's wealth was rampant. It has been estimated that by 1947 the fortunes amassed by the big bureaucratic families of Chang Kai-shek (蒋介石), T. V. Soong (宋子文), H. H. Kung (孔祥熙) and the Chen brothers (Chen Lifu 〈陈立夫〉 and Chen Guofu 〈陈果夫〉) totalled somewhere between U. S. $10 and U. S. $20 billion, accounting for 80 percent of the country's industrial capital. A large part of their property and wealth were scattered in the United States, Western Europe and South America.

According to American writer Sterling Seagrave in his book *The Soong Dynasty*, toward the end of the Anti-Japanese War "the Kungs and Soongs all along had spread some of their fortune around South America, including what were reputed to be megalithic deposits in Caracas, Buenos Aires, and Sao Paulo banks. Their holdings reportedly covered a broad spectrum of oil, minerals, shipping, and other transportation stocks, with heaviest emphasis on rails and airlines vital in a continent of great distances and few roads. "

He also wrote in the same book that a friend of T. V. Soong was quoted as saying that T. V. Soong's assets in the United States alone were over U. S. $ 47 million by 1944. In 1949, allegations by banking sources to members of the U. S. Congress showed that the Soongs and Kungs actually had $ 2 billion salted away in Manhattan.

The U. S. Federal Bureau of Investigation made a secret investigation, but no findings were disclosed. It was reported that Madame Chiang Kai-shek had $ 150 million deposited in the Chase National Bank and National City Bank in New York or one of them; T. V. Soong had $ 70 million and Madame Kung had $ 80 million in one or the other of these two banks.

Imperialism and feudalism in China were by no means harmful to these people. In order to safeguard its vested interests, the Kuomintang leading clique rejected a democratic coalition government in favor of a civil war. At the beginning of the war, they believed they could win by relying on their superiority in manpower, equipment and strategic advantages, as well as the support of the United States. If they had won, China would have remained a semi-colonial and semi-feudal country.

Why did the Kuomintang meet with disastrous failure in the civil war it itself launched? It is because it went against the will of the people. Not only were workers, peasants and students against it, a majority of intellectuals like university professors and most national industrialists and business people also opposed it.

We may say that many people who had expected China to take the capitalist road abandoned the Kuomintang, for they had perceived that such a bureaucrat-capitalist force, in league with the feudal landlord class and relying on foreign imperialists, could not lead China along the road of independent, free capitalism. The utter isolation of the Kuomintang among the Chinese people rendered its failure inevitable. A historical pattern was thus determined: In China it was impossible for any force representing the bourgeoisie to complete a democratic revolution.

## IV

China did not embark on the capitalist road, because in semi-colonial and semi-feudal China, except for the Communist Party, there was no other political party or political force that could solve China's problems: independence (freedom from the rule and oppression of imperialism), land reform (emancipating peasants from the feudal land-based relationship), and democracy and unification. The last problem was directly related to the first two; without solving them there could be neither democratization of the state nor real unification of the country.

All political forces in old China, except the Communist Party, suppressed the worker and peasant masses and were afraid of fully mobilizing the masses, or were unable to mobilize them. So, these political forces either attached themselves to imperialism or feared imperialist forces. Without mobilizing the broad masses of workers, peasants and petty bourgeoisie and without uniting all forces that could be united, it would have been impossible to overcome the powerful imperialists and domestic reactionary forces backed by the imperialists.

The Chinese Communist Party alone had achieved this through such mobilization. Peasants, the overwhelming majority of China's population, constituted the largest force in desperate need of revolution. At the same time they were backward in certain respects because of their economic and cultural backgrounds. How to mobilize this force along the right path was the key question for success of China's democratic revolution. Only the Communist Party was ready to answer it.

The fact that China's democratic revolution was achieved under the leadership of the Communist Party with workers, peasants and petty bourgeoisie as its main forces ruled out the possibility of establishing a bourgeoisie-dominated state after the revolution, and therefore ruled out capitalism.

Let us suppose at the point of victory in 1949 the Communist Party had handed leadership to the capitalist forces; where then would China have gone? Tasks for democratic revolution which were only half completed at the time could not have been fulfilled, and this would have aroused the resentment of the masses of workers, peasants and petty bourgeoisie, and created the sort of disruption in which capitalism could not develop peacefully. If the Kuomintang had staged a comeback, the imperialists would have seized the opportunity to intrude and China would have returned to its semi-colonial, semi-feudal position.

It was also impossible for the Communist Party to create a socialist country directly after the victory of the new-democratic revolution. The Communist Party understood that subjective desire alone could not bring about socialism and that to eventually reach socialism via a new-democratic revolution was the only practical way forward.

On the eve of nationwide victory in 1949, the Communist Party declared its three major economic intentions: 1) confiscate the land of the feudal class and turn it over to the peasants, 2) confiscate monopoly capital or bureaucratic capital owned by Kuomintang reactionary rulers and turn it over to the new-democratic state, and 3) protect the industry and commerce of the national bourgeoisie.

The state-owned economy of the new-democratic state was the first of the socialist economic elements, and it took the lead in the whole national economy. Mao Zedong said that "bureaucratic capital has prepared ample material conditions for the new-democratic revolution," adding, "in view of China's economic backwardness, even after the country-wide victory of the revolution, it will still be necessary to permit existence for a long time of a capitalist sector of the economy represented by the extensive upper petty bourgeoisie and middle bourgeoisie. In accordance with the division of labor in the national economy, a certain development of all parts of this capitalist sector which are beneficial to the national economy will still be needed. This capitalist sector will still be an indispensable part of the whole national economy."[1]

With the elimination of imperialist privileges, the

---

[ 1 ] Mao Zedong, *The Present Situation and Our Tasks*, December 1947.

overthrow of bureaucratic capitalism, and the completion of land reform throughout China, national capital
was in a better position to develop than was ever the
case in old China. Of course, it could not grow as it
would in capitalist countries.

The *Common Program of the People's Political Consultative Conference* (人民政协纲领) enacted after the
founding of the People's Republic of China noted: "The
People's Government shall encourage active operation of
all private economic enterprises beneficial to the national
welfare and to the people's livelihood and shall assist in
their development.... When necessary and possible,
private capital shall be encouraged to develop in the direction of state capitalism."

This makes it clear that growth of private capital
would be valued within a context of society's overall
benefit and that its direction would be guided away from
the norm in capitalist countries.

Perhaps some people would ask whether the country could simply practice new democracy without going
on to socialism. It is impossible. In the new-democratic
society there was already a sector of socialist economy—
the state-run economy. (There were very few socialist
cooperatives at the time.) The private capitalist economy could not survive without the support of the state
and without maintaining ties with the state economy. It
would then evolve naturally into state capitalism.

In 1956, with the basic completion of socialist
transformation of agriculture, handcrafts, and capitalist
industry and commerce, China made the transition from
new democracy to socialism, more quickly than esti-
mates foresaw in 1952-53. The inevitability of this
smooth transformation is rooted in the situation of the

time. It testifies to the truth that the Party and state policies were consistent with objective needs.

Some people would say that since China did not go through the capitalist period, it is unsuitable for China to build a socialist society. This view is not right. It is true that China did not go through an independent stage of capitalism, to say nothing of more developed stages of capitalism. China's history would not allow that.

But China did go through capitalism in a special way. Though we can not equate a semi-colonial and semi-feudal China with a capitalist society, it is also a fact that capitalist elements did exist in China at the time (capital of foreign imperialists, bureaucratic capital and national capital). These produced the proletariat, the bourgeoisie and the petty bourgeoisie in China. Without them there could not have been the proletariat-led new-democratic revolution or the social transition from new democracy to socialism.

Others hold that China has lost a lot because it did not go through a developed capitalist stage. Soon after China embarked onto the socialist road it met with difficulties and made mistakes, all of which were due to China's economic and cultural backwardness, called "being poor and blank." That backwardness was due to China never having gone through the developed capitalist stage. If this is a "loss" we have suffered, we can but endure it.

Since history did not allow us a developed capitalist stage, we have to skip it and set to building a socialist society on the given basis of "being poor and blank."

Modern history in China has allowed only two paths for the Chinese people: one was to be continuously reduced to a colony and dependency on imperialists (This would be the reality if the Communist Party could not lead the Chinese people to wage resolute struggle, or if it failed because the method used in the struggle was wrong); the other was the socialist road which we have actually already taken by going through the new-democratic revolution.

Did China have any other choices? Even if China could start with very underdeveloped capitalism, international circumstances would not allow it to become an independent underdeveloped capitalist country, much less progress to a developed capitalist country. One can imagine how many social contradictions and class conflicts there would be, how many hardships the Chinese people would have to suffer and how much blood they would have to shed.

If China, huge and backward as it is, trudged the capitalist road, one could see a repeat of the situation in old China where hundreds of millions of people went homeless, millions of poor people starved to death and millions of women became prostitutes.

Therefore, it was not a "loss" for China to overcome its semi-colonial and semi-feudal status and move on from new democracy to socialism. For China, the capitalist road would be very long and hopeless, littered with hardship and setback, and probably filled with bloodshed and revolution.

We have been on the socialist road for thirty years and more and have encountered many difficulties and made many mistakes. But we have made much headway in developing China's economy and culture, which would not have happened if we had taken the capitalist road.

People have a dynamic role to play in promoting development of their histories, but they are absolutely in no position to arbitrarily construct the road their country takes. All they can do is to choose from whatever paths history makes available to them. The road the Chinese people chose is the best they had.

## V

Some say because China has not undergone the developed capitalist stage, China should abandon socialism and make up the missed stage. The fallacy of this argument has already been demonstrated.

However, if the argument is that we must learn from the useful experiences many countries have learned under capitalism, experiences which are necessary for socialism, then it is right.

Here I would like to explain the relation between capitalism and socialism. Only by wiping out the capitalist ownership which rules a capitalist society can we have public ownership of socialism. Socialism and capitalism oppose each other. On the other hand, the materialist base that will eventually abolish private ownership is the large-scale socialized production shaped by capitalism. When the proletariat overthrows the rule of the bourgeoisie, it should inherit and make use of large-scale socialized production to build socialism. In other words, socialism and capitalism are linked by a hereditary relationship. Here lies the basic reason why socialism can only be reached through capitalism. Marx and Engels said, "History is nothing but the succession of the separate generations, each of which uses the materials, the capital funds, the productive forces handed down to it by all preceding generations. . . . "[1] It cannot but be the same for a socialist society inheriting the capitalist society.

V. I. Lenin once declared that a capitalist society prepared many ready-made conditions for socialism. "Capitalism has created an accounting apparatus in the shape of banks, syndicates, postal service, consumers' societies, and office employees' unions," he said. "Without big banks socialism would be impossible."

" 'State apparatus'. . . which we may take ready-made from capitalism; our task here is merely to lop off what capitalistically mutilates this excellent apparatus, to make it even bigger, even more democratic, even more comprehensive."[2]

Under the socialist system, public ownership is able to develop in the interest of the people large-scale socialized production inherited from the old society in a way impermissible under the capitalist system. Here lies the superiority of the socialist system. However, realization of that possibility in different countries entails different processes and lengths of time.

The richer the "heritage" from capitalism the better for socialist construction. Theoretically, it should be easier to build socialism in a developed capitalist country after the victory of its proletarian revolution. However, once capitalism had dominated the world, production level was only one of the factors to determine which capitalist countries would be the first to break from capitalism.

---

[1]  Karl Marx and Frederick Engels, *Collected Works*, New York, International Publishers, 1976, Vol. V, p. 50.
[2]  V. I. Lenin, *Collected Works*, Moscow, Progress Publishers, Vol. 26.

Other factors such as international conditions, relative strengths of domestic classes, and development of the class struggle became more relevant. The fact is, since the October Revolution in 1917, those that have entered the socialist stage are not the most developed capitalist countries.

Lenin pointed out that because Russia was the most backward country in Europe it had difficulties after its revolution. He said, "It was easier for the Russians than for the advanced countries to begin the great proletarian revolution, but it will be more difficult for them to continue it and carry it to final victory, in the sense of the complete organization of a socialist society. "[1]

After the October Revolution in 1917 there appeared "Left-wing Communists" who regarded all things related to bourgeoisie as incompatible with socialism and thought these must be abandoned. To counter such a childish view, Lenin said that "Socialism is impossible unless it makes use of the achievements of the engineering and culture created by large-scale capitalism. "[2]

He repeated, "Socialism cannot be built unless we utilize the heritage of capitalist culture. The only material we have to build communism with is what has been left us by capitalism. "[3]

Therefore, Lenin stressed repeatedly that once the tasks of socialist revolution had been achieved, it was imperative to learn from organizers of trusts and from entrepreneurs and businessmen experienced in large-scale production.

---

[ 1 ]  *Ibid.* , Vol. 29.
[ 2 ]  *Ibid.* , Vol. 27.
[ 3 ]  *Ibid.* , Vol. 29.

Lenin said, "We shall now learn from them because we lack knowledge, because we do not have this knowledge. We know about socialism, but knowledge of organization on a scale of millions, knowledge of the organization and distribution of goods and so on — this we do not have. The old Bolshevik leaders did not teach us this. The Bolshevik Party cannot boast of this in its history. We have not done a course on this yet. And we say, let him be a thorough-paced rascal even, but if he has organized a trust, if he is a merchant who has dealt with the organization of production and distribution for millions and tens of millions, if he has acquired experience — we must learn from him. If we do not learn this from them, we shall not get socialism, the revolution will remain at the stage it has now reached."[1]

When the Chinese revolution was crowned with victory, Mao Zedong made a similar point. He said in 1949, "The serious task of economic construction lies before us. We shall soon put aside some of the things we know well and be compelled to do things we don't know well. This means difficulties."

He added, "We must overcome difficulties, we must learn what we do not know. We must learn to do economic work from all who know how, no matter who they are. We must esteem them as teachers, learning from them respectfully and conscientiously. We must not pretend to know what we do not know. We must not put on bureaucratic airs."[2]

Undoubtedly, what Mao Zedong said here is correct.

---

[1] *Ibid.*, Vol. 27.
[2] Mao Zedong, *On the People's Democratic Dictatorship.*

As mentioned above, we cannot say that no capitalist heritage was left by old China but that heritage was indeed minimal.

In a country with a poor economic foundation, but with historical conditions which enable the proletariat to lead the people in socialist revolution and socialist construction, the proletariat should not retreat. The Communist Party of China has not flinched from any difficulty.

However, the proletariat must be realistic about the difficulties engendered by the poor capitalist "legacy," and must adopt various kinds of transitional economic forms on its way. It must study what capitalism has to teach about organizing large-scale production, including science, technology and managerial expertise.

Unfortunately, in China's socialist construction this was neglected for a long time, and learning from capitalist experience was wrongly considered a violation of socialist principles.

In the past thirty years, China has become economically stronger. But we admit that we are still in the initial stage of socialism. After the Third Plenary Session of the Eleventh Party Central Committee in 1978, we broke the yoke of the earlier rigid concept of socialist patterns, and carried out economic structural reform to enliven the economy in both urban and rural areas.

For example, in the countryside, we instituted the contract responsibility system with remuneration linked to production. In combining the planned economy and the commodity economy, we strive for the full development of the commodity economy and take various kinds of private enterprises as supplements to the state sector.

These measures are proof that we do not refuse to

learn from economic experience of past class societies, especially of capitalist countries. However, this does not mean we are making up the missed stage of capitalism. On the contrary, what we have adopted are policies and methods conforming to China's concrete conditions at its early socialist stage.

In this early stage, opening to the outside world is of special significance. The *Decision of the CPC Central Committee on Reform of the Economic Structure* adopted in 1984 states, "We must draw on the world's advanced methods of management, including those of developed capitalist countries, that conform to the laws of modern, socialized production."

The *Resolution of the CPC Central Committee on the Guiding Principles for Building a Socialist Society with an Advanced Culture and Ideology* adopted in 1986 also states, "We should do our utmost to learn from all countries, including the developed capitalist countries, to acquire advanced science and technology, universally applicable expertise in economic management and administrative work and other useful knowledge and to verify and develop in practice what we have learned."

Aside from other reasons, opening to the outside world is important precisely because there is so much we need to learn in the process of building socialism. In this we cannot and need not take the capitalist road. We can learn faster and better under a socialist system — this is the first conclusion I have come to in this article.

We need to learn what is useful. We will resolutely reject the capitalist ideological and social systems that defend exploitation and oppression, as well as all dark and decadent aspects of capitalism. This is my second conclusion.

The socialist system has thrust deep roots into the land of China. Although it is still young, it has displayed exuberant vitality. Socialism will not grow spontaneously. If we are good at cultivating it, it will certainly grow into a towering tree. This is my third conclusion.

(Written in February 1987 and first Published in *People's Daily*, 1 March 1987 )

# Several Problems Related to Modern China and the World*

The topic of this international symposium is "Modern China and the World", a topic that covers a wide range of subjects. Scholars present at the symposium will discuss relevant questions from various perspectives and there may be different opinions on the same subject. It is my belief that the exchange of views from different angles among scholars will be useful for deepening the discussion and the exploration of relevant questions.

I would like to say something on this topic here.

The modern history of China commenced with the British war of aggression against China, or the Opium War, between 1840 and 1842. At that time, Chinese feudal society, which had lasted for more than 2,000 years, was on the wane and change was brewing in society. Economically, the seeds of capitalist relations of production, such as handicraft workshops, appeared, and politically there was suspicion of and protest against the feudal autocratic tradition. The arrival of the aggressive forces of Western capitalism, heralded by their gun-boat diplomacy, greatly influenced the direction of social development in China.

In modern times, China was bullied by all the imperialist nations, both great and small. Several of the major powers divided up spheres of influence in China and some even tried to monopolize this occupation of the country. This period of history began in 1840 and lasted for 109 years. Before 1840, China was almost completely cut off from the outside world, the rest of the world knew little about China and vice versa. After 1840, China began to have more and more contact with other countries. This occurred in numerous fields and in various forms, but the main contacts involved armed aggression, economic plundering and political subjugation of China by the imperialist powers. China was humiliated, its people slaughtered and its interests violated.

Foreign aggression and oppression were bound to evoke opposition from the Chinese people. China has a long cultural tradition and a long history as a unified state. The aggression and exploitation of the capitalist nations therefore met with strong resistance from the very start. With the appearance on the Chinese social stage of the bourgeoisie and the proletariat, the struggle against imperialism and its lackeys and agents grew even more vigorous. Under pressure from the imperialist powers, some areas of China were colonized and the nation's sovereignty was infringed upon; as a result, China became a semi-independent, i.e., a semi-colonial state. However, China was not completely reduced to a colony thanks to the resistance of the Chinese people, the expansion and growth of which eventually saved China from becoming a colony or a semi-colony, secured national independence, and restored full sovereignty to the nation. The modern history of China is therefore also a history of the opposition of the Chinese people to capitalist and imperialist aggression and oppression.

Imperialist aggression, plundering and exploitation resulted in China's poverty and backwardness in modern times. It should be pointed out here that the control of

China's economic lifelines and politics by the imperialist powers was the reason why the seeds of capitalism in Chinese feudal society did not take root and grow, and why China did not enter the stage of capitalism. It is true that the foreign capitalist invasion had a destructive effect on the foundation of the Chinese natural economy, and boosted the development of a commodity economy and capitalist elements, but the Chinese national capital that emerged in the middle of last century was kept in extreme difficulties and was not able to develop vigorously. It was not only oppressed by foreign capital with a variety of privileges, but was also incapable of resisting the pre-capitalist system of exploitation that still predominated in Chinese society. The Qing court still ruled during the first seventy years of modern Chinese history, and the imperialists made it a docile tool. After the collapse of the Qing dynasty, the imperialists supported the warlord bureaucrats who represented the interests of the landlord class, and the comprador bourgeoisie. Feudal land relationships, commercial usurers, and the pre-capitalist system of exploitation and its superstructure were all able to continue with the support of the imperialists, who used them as instruments for ruling and exploiting the Chinese people. Imperialist aggression thus blocked the way to an industrial and democratic China, and reduced China to the status of a semicolonial, semi-feudal society.

Modern China was not a modernized China, not an industrial and democratic country with a developed economy and education. There were two problems that confronted modern China: one problem was how to cast off the yoke of imperialist control and oppression and make China an independent country; the other was how to make China modernized. Obviously the two problems were closely interrelated. China was bullied because it lagged behind, and because it was frequently bullied it lagged even further behind. A vicious cycle.

Was it possible to realize modernization first and then break away from this vicious cycle? In a semi-colonial and semi-feudal nation, all efforts to save China through stimulating industry and education, or to realize democratization and modernization through legitimate means, were doomed to failure. The well-wishers who devoted themselves to invigorating national industries and education achieved some success, but they did not attain the goal of making China modernized, independent and powerful. Even more useless were the attempts at democratization while maintaining the existing political and social order intact. The forceful obstruction of the imperialists and their agents was responsible for the failure of these good intentions.

It was very difficult to first win national independence. Given the very backward social foundation, it was of course not easy to defeat the imperialist forces who were already in a predominant position in China. However, historical experience demonstrated that only this could save China from the vicious cycle, i. e. , the construction of a modern political system, economy and culture could be considered only after China had won national liberation and independence.

Contradictions between the imperialist powers in their aggression towards China and between their agents could be made use of by the Chinese people in their struggle for liberation and independence. But the problem of major importance was how to mobilize and unite all the anti-imperialist forces. Under the leadership of the Communist Party of China the Chinese people, after a long and arduous struggle, finally accomplished their historical mission, liberating China from the fetters of imperialism and opening up a broad road to modernization in the country.

The above is the first point I wish to make.

Was modern China open to the outside world?

This may have seemed unquestionable, but in fact it was not the case.

In semi-colonial China, even when there was no foreign military aggression, foreigners had a variety of privileges based on unequal treaties with China, and the key to the nation's door was in the hands of foreigners (i. e. , the Chinese customs were under their control). They could freely establish banks, commercial houses and factories in China, imperialist gunboats and commercial vessels sailed freely along the Chinese coast and inland rivers, and imperialist troops were stationed on Chinese soil. The Chinese government was at the beck and call of its imperialist bosses when foreign policies and even important domestic policies were decided. Under these circumstances, how could there be any national seclusion to speak of?

Around 1900, the American government initiated an open door policy, but it did not call for the opening of China's door to the rest of the world because this had already been burst open. This policy was actually directed against the spheres of influence of other imperialist powers and was a statement of the principle of "the protection of equal privileges" for all the imperialist powers. The American policy stipulated that the spheres of influence belonging to any power should be open to all other powers and should not be made inaccessible to them.

Although modern China was controlled by the imperialist powers politically and economically, the latter were nevertheless unsatisfied with the situation in China. Generally speaking, their dissatisfaction centered around the following two points:

Politically, the imperialist powers believed that the agents they used to rule China were not strong enough to safeguard their interests in the face of opposition from the Chinese people; they could not defuse such opposition and were often beaten down by it. This question will not, however, be discussed in detail here. Obviously this was a contradiction created by the imperialists themselves. Since the forces supported by the foreign powers did not serve the interests of the Chinese people and nation, they naturally did not enjoy prestige among the people and could not maintain the domestic stability favorable to imperialism, although these forces had "legitimate" political power and a strong army.

Economically, the imperialists were dissatisfied with China's failure to become a vast commodity market, a good place for investment, and a large supplier of raw materials, which they had expected when they forced China's door open with their gunboats. China's total volume of imports and exports in 1936 (the year before the final outbreak of the War of Resistance Against Japan) was only an insignificant 1. 6 billion yuan (US $ 500 million at the current exchange rate), an increase of less than 30% over the figure for 1910. In the seventy years following the Opium Wars, China's largest import was opium. Until the eve of the founding of New China, China's main imports were kerosene, sugar, cotton cloth and cheap manufactured goods, while its exports were limited to "traditional" commodities such as raw silk, bristles, tungsten ore and tung oil. The imperialist nations invested rather heavily in China. According to economists' estimates, the imperialists' investments in China rose from US \$ 1. 5 billion at the beginning of the twentieth century to US \$ 4. 3 billion in the year before the War of Resistance Against Japan. During this period, investments made by the imperialist powers were predatory in nature, and the imperialists were able to make maximum profits as a result of their privileges. These investments did not involve the use of their own capital, since, for the most part, investments came from the "indemnities" paid by China, the remainder being acquired from the land they occupied in China through extortion (real estate was the major source of foreign capital in cities like Shanghai), profits from the opium trade, and the savings of the Chinese people in foreign banks. In short, the major part of their huge capital investment was money plundered or earned in China. China's mineral resources remained buried deep in the ground and were not tapped.

Why did China, with its door wide open, not become a vast market? The answer is very simple: China was too poor and backward.

Being poor and backward, China did not have huge quantities of surplus products for export and could not afford to buy in large quantities of goods from abroad. The imperialist economic invasion reached sections of the countryside, but most rural areas were still at the stage of a natural or semi-natural economy, and had no commodity economy or only a trace. Rural areas that contained the majority of the Chinese population were therefore not actually open to the outside world. True, coastal areas were open to other countries, but Shanghai was known as "a paradise for adventurers" where foreign hooligans, swindlers and smugglers could become rich quickly and illegally, and normal trade inevitably diminished.

During the course of China's modern history, there were numerous boycotts of goods from America, Britain and Japan, with Chinese merchants and urban residents taking an active role. Such movements embodied the hatred harbored by the Chinese people towards the aggressors and testified to the fact that the economic opening-up that took place during that period only brought misery to Chinese people and society.

Such poverty and backwardness was brought about by imperialism. It could be said, on the one hand, that the imperialist powers broke through China's doors and forced the nation to open to the outside world; on the other hand, their plundering and exploitation kept China poor and backward, and unable to open in the true sense. This was another contradiction the imperialist powers created but could not resolve.

In the 1930s and 1940s, it was stated in the Chinese press that the imperialist powers should consider ways of helping China to become strong and prosperous because only a strong and prosperous China would be able to greatly increase its trade and economic transactions with them. While the second half of this statement is correct, the first half is wrong since it was only a dream to count on the imperialist powers to help China become strong and prosperous.

Only after China won national independence and regained national sovereignty through the efforts of its own people could it develop its economy and open its door to the rest of the world as an independent state, and on the basis of equality and mutual benefit. This has been borne out by the facts.

This is the second point I wish to make.

My third point is that this aggression and oppression reduced China to a poor, backward nation. On the one hand, this caused great suffering for the Chinese people, and on the other, a poor, backward China became a destabilizing factor in the world.

The imperialist powers scrambled for rights and interests in China and came into frequent conflict with one another. By the beginning of the 20th century, the contending powers in China were primarily Britain, Germany, Russia and France, with Britain and Russia as the main adversaries. There was no open hostility between the four powers, but in 1904 war broke out on China's soil between Russia and the newly emerging Japan over the domination of Northeast China. Later, after the First World War, Britain, the United States and Japan fought for control of China. The conflict between the imperialist powers over China was reflected in the confused battles among the Chinese warlords, which pushed China into even greater turmoil. Japan grew confident in the 1930s that it could make use of the internal situation in China to monopolize control of the country. The opposition between Japan and the United States after 1931 eventually led to the Pacific War between Japan on one side and the United States and Britain on the other. Japan's aggression towards China triggered off the war in East Asia, which constituted part of the Second World War.

Historical experience has shown that this imperialist aggression and oppression reduced China, a big country with a large population comprising one fifth to a quarter of the world's total, to a poor, weak, semi-colonial state, thereby creating a focus for international contradictions and conflicts.

Through their own efforts, the Chinese people have transformed China into an independent and stable socialist country with a gradually developing economy. This is a failure for the imperialist forces who tried to invade and even exclusively dominate China, but it is a contribution to world peace and stability. Only when China is no longer a bone of contention among the imperialist powers can it coexist peacefully with other countries, contribute to peace and stability in East Asia and the Pacific, and become a positive factor for peace and stability throughout the world. I believe that this is the only conclusion to be drawn from a comparison of Chinese history after 1949 with that in the one hundred years before 1949.

* A speech given at the *International Symposium on Modern China and the World* held in Beijing.

(First published in *People's Daily*, 17 October, 1990)

# China's Reform and Opening to the Outside World

## —A Speech Delivered at the Asia University in Japan

1992 will see the 20th anniversary of the normalization of diplomatic relations between China and Japan, which took place in 1972. It was an epoch-making event in the history of relations between the two countries. Since that time, friendship and cooperation between the two countries and peoples has developed steadily and in an all-round way, in spite of this or that difficulty. It is the common desire of both peoples to maintain their friendship from generation to generation. The further development of this friendship and cooperation depends on deepening the mutual understanding between the two peoples and the academic circles of the two countries. Many people in Japan know and study China. This is very good.

I will now avail myself of this opportunity to talk to you about China's reform and opening to the outside world. This is a very big question, and I would like to explain, in the light of historical development, why China has initiated the policy of reform and opening-up and adopted it as one of the nation's basic policies.

# I

China's policy of reform and opening to the outside world is closely related to its adherence to socialism. China's reform is being carried out within the framework of the socialist system, as is the nation's opening-up. Therefore, before elaborating on the reform and opening-up, I would like to explain briefly why China embarked upon the socialist road and continues to adhere to socialism, also in the light of historical development.

As far back as the early 1920s, there was debate in Chinese intellectual circles on whether China should take a capitalist or a socialist road. At that time, one group believed that China was incapable of taking the socialist road, although the socialist system was superior to the capitalist system, and in order to solve its problems of poverty and backwardness China could only develop capitalism. The other group believed that international and domestic conditions made it impossible for China to develop capitalism independently and therefore China had no other alternative but socialism. In retrospect, the view that China could not directly embark on a socialist road was correct, but historical facts have demonstrated that it was impractical to try to independently develop capitalism.

Whether China took a capitalist or a socialist road was not determined by which of the two was superior. It should be admitted that many of those who advocated a capitalist road in the years before the 1920s and between the 1920s and 1940s were striving for China's progress and development.

China was a backward, semi-colonial, semi-feudal society and it would have been progress if the nation had embarked independently on a capitalist road. However, the problem was that given the historical conditions at that time it was impossible for China to develop capitalism independently since there were no bourgeois forces capable of creating the preconditions for the development of capitalism. What were these preconditions?

Firstly, independence. When China suffered aggression and oppression at the hands of almost all the imperialist powers in the world and lost its sovereignty and independence, there was no development of national capitalism to speak of.

Secondly, unity. Social contradictions, especially the rivalry among the warlords backed by imperialist powers, led to continuous civil wars and disintegration of the country. In such circumstances realization of national unity had to precede the development of capitalism.

Thirdly, reform of the land system. There was no capitalism to speak of when Chinese peasants, who comprised more than eighty per cent of the total population, had little or no land and lived a miserable life under the yoke of pre-capitalism. There was a widespread call for democracy in China at that time, but the essential content of democracy was the right of hundreds of millions of the peasants to survival and democracy.

China was bound to have met with strong resistance from hostile forces if it had tried to achieve independence and unity and to carry out reform of the land system. The national bourgeoisie was too weak to mobilize the broad masses in order to wage a victorious struggle. One can see this clearly from the fact that Dr. Sun Yat-sen had to cooperate with the newly emerging Communist Party when he genuinely and sincerely tried to create the preconditions for developing capitalism.

The other group involved in the debate in the early 1920s were China's early Marxists. They rightly concluded that China was not able to develop capitalism independently, but they wrongly believed that socialism was imminent. They very soon realized that the current task was not to strive for socialism, but to achieve independence, unity and carry out land reform—the tasks of the national democratic revolution. The Chinese Communist Party bravely shouldered the responsibilities that the bourgeoisie were unable to shoulder, mobilized the broad masses of peasants as well as the workers, students, intellectuals and all other sectors of the patriotic forces and, after an extremely hard and bitter struggle, brought the national democratic revolution to a successful conclusion in 1949. We call the revolution that achieved victory in 1949 the new democratic revolution to differentiate it from the old democratic revolution led by the bourgeoisie. The victory of the latter would have led to the founding of a capitalist state while the victory of the former inevitably brought China onto the socialist road.

The national capitalists in old China lacked strength; some of them took an active part in the new democratic revolution led by the Communist Party, some remained neutral, and some went to Hong Kong, Taiwan or abroad on the eve of the nationwide victory of the revolution for understandable reasons. The government of New China adopted a policy of protecting the national industry and commerce, which both achieved unprecedented growth in the new democratic nation.

However, the bourgeoisie did not play a significant role in either economic or political life. In the 1950s, China carried out a socialist transformation of capitalist industry and commerce by means of a peaceful buying-out policy, and at the same time individual peasants who had received land in the land reform were organized into socialist cooperatives. China was thus ushered into socialism.

Was it necessary for China to embark on the socialist road in the 1950s? It was impossible for China to take the capitalist road because there it lacked a powerful bourgeoisie. As can be seen from the experience of various countries, the development of capitalism relied externally on the plundering of colonies and internally on the exploitation of peasants and other small producers, reducing them to abject poverty. China could not and should not have plundered other countries. If China had exploited the peasants and other small producers there would have been new class polarizations among the hundreds of millions of Chinese people and long-lasting social disturbances and unrest, with the result that China would have been reduced to a semi-colonial and semi-feudal society rather than developing capitalism.

As a matter of fact, in spite of detours and difficulties in the past 30-odd years since China took the socialist road, China has maintained its national independence, unity and social stability, its economy has developed, and people's lives have been generally improved. All this could not have been accomplished if China had followed the capitalist road.

Socialism was therefore a historical necessity for China under its specific conditions. It was also an unprecedented feat that China, starting from a semi-colonial, semi-feudal society, won victory in the new democratic revolution and finally headed towards socialism. It is indeed extremely difficult to construct socialism on a backward economic and social base, hence the initiation of reform and opening to the outside world.

## II

The policy of reform was implemented after 1978, but it can be traced back to the early years of socialist construction in China.

When China began its own socialist construction it had only the experience of the Soviet Union during its first 30-odd years to refer to and learn from. After three years of economic recovery after 1949, China immediately inaugurated the First Five-Year Plan (1953-57). The socialist transformation of capitalist industry, commerce and agriculture during this period had unique Chinese characteristics and was not copied from the Soviet Union. However, Soviet influence was obvious in its economic construction.

At that time, Chinese leaders began to see that the Soviet experience should not be copied. In his 1956 speech *On the Ten Major Relationships* (论十大关系)in which he discussed China's socialist construction, Mao Zedong firmly pointed out that China should draw lessons from Soviet defects and errors, which he listed as follows:

Firstly, the Soviet Union and some Eastern European countries placed "lop-sided stress on heavy industry to the neglect of agriculture and light industry".

Secondly, in terms of the relationship between the state and the peasants, "the Soviet Union has adopted measures which squeeze the peasants very hard", and "the Soviet Union made grave mistakes on this question".

Thirdly, "We must not follow the example of the Soviet Union in concentrating everything in the hands of the central authorities, shackling the local authorities and denying them the right to independent action".

Fourthly, "In the Soviet Union the relationship between the Russian nationality and the minority nationalities is very abnormal".

Fifthly, in China "many democratic parties with the national bourgeoisie and its intellectuals as the main body still exist. In this respect, China is different from the Soviet Union".

Sixthly, Mao Zedong proposed "learning from other countries. " He said, "At present the leaders of some countries are chary and even afraid of advancing this slogan". He did not mention the country by name, but obviously he was referring to the Soviet Union.

In addition Mao Zedong touched on the independent action of factories under the centralized leadership, saying that "It's not right, I'm afraid, to place everything in the hands of the central or the provincial and municipal authorities without leaving the factories any power of their own, any room for independent action, any benefit". Here he was also alluding to the Soviet experience.

In retrospect, Mao Zedong did not see very clearly the drawbacks of the Soviet model, but he was aware of some of its major problems. Of course, seeing the defects of the Soviet model did not mean finding the right way. However, from the late 1950s the Chinese leadership adopted a clear guiding principle that China should not copy the Soviet model and must take a road suited to the realities of China.

From the end of the 1950s the contradictions between the two countries began to intensify. In the 1960s there were disagreements between the two parties that led to the breaking off of relations. Relations between the two countries existed only in a nominal way and eventually military conflicts took place along the border. This precarious state of affairs lasted for nearly thirty years until 1989 when normal relations were restored, although they were still not as good as those of the 1950s.

Numerous factors were responsible for the break in relations between China and the Soviet Union, but the main reason was that China did not follow the Soviet baton in its external and internal policies and refused to be one of its "satellite states". China was determined to blaze a new socialist path suited to its specific conditions.

As mentioned above, from the very beginning China differed in some respects from the Soviet Union in its socialist construction. China always attached great importance to agriculture; it did not abolish non-Communist democratic parties, but practiced a system of multi-party cooperation and political consultation under the leadership of the Communist Party, not one-party politics. China also differed from the Soviet Union in its handling of the relationship with minority nationalities. China has also sometimes made mistakes in these respects, but generally speaking it has done a good job.

The fundamental defect of the Soviet model lay in its economic structure whereby the state took care of everything and shouldered too heavy a load. This economic structure excluded a commodity economy, hindered the growth of various social activities and led to rigidity. Although such a structure was very disadvantageous when maintained over a long period of time, it was effective within a limited period and was therefore difficult to abolish immediately when a backward country started socialist construction.

Mao Zedong's emphasis in his speech *On the Ten Major Relationships* on bringing the initiative of the local authorities into full play and giving enterprises greater room for independent actions was aimed at the defects of the Soviet economic structure. But China was also prone to such drawbacks in its socialist construction if it could not find a correct way under the specific historical conditions.

China is an Eastern agricultural nation, large and backward, and unlike any of the European states. During its socialist construction there were no ready-made experiences for China to copy, nor could there have been. China therefore had to make an independent search, on the basis of practice, for a new road of its own.

During the long years of revolutionary struggle, China accumulated rich experiences and forged its own traditions, which were undoubtedly useful in its search for the correct socialist road. However, these experiences and traditions had to be integrated with the practice of its socialist construction. In *On the Ten Major Relationships* Mao Zedong proposed the basic policy of "mobilizing all positive factors, internal and external, to serve the cause of socialism". He said, "In the past we followed this policy of mobilizing all positive factors in order to put an end to the rule of imperialism, feudalism and bureaucrat-capitalism and to win victory for the people's democratic revolution. We are now following the same policy in order to carry on the socialist revolution and build a socialist country. "This policy is undoubtedly correct, but how can all positive factors be mobilized in socialist construction, and what mechanisms and methods should be employed—these constitute a very complex new problem.

From the late 1950s onwards, China made every effort for twenty successive years to find its own road of socialist construction, during the course of which two major mistakes were made. The first was in 1958 when it launched the "Great Leap Forward"（大跃进）movement which resulted in a three-year period of serious economic difficulties. The people's communes（人民公社）established in rural areas at about the same time also proved to be a failure. The second was the "cultural revolution"（文化大革命）, which lasted for ten years from 1966. I cannot discuss in detail here the mistakes of the "Great Leap Forward", the people's communes and the "cultural revolution". To put it briefly, these mistakes were made when the Chinese leadership depended too heavily on the experiences of mass struggle and class struggle gained over the preceding years of revolution in an attempt to break away from the rigid Soviet model, and wrongly believed that a mass movement in production and on the political front would enhance social vitality and spur economic development. China did make considerable progress in its economic development during that period, but at great cost as a result of these mistakes.

Although these twenty years were riddled with mistakes and detours they were not frittered away. It could be said that China began to make attempts at reform, that is, the search for its own road of socialist construction, as early as the late 1950s. The mistakes made during this period taught us many lessons. Of course, some mistakes could have been avoided, but it was certainly very difficult for China, given its specific conditions, to find the correct road for building socialism and it was almost impossible to find such a road without any detours or defeats. The mistakes of the "Great Leap Forward" and the "cultural revolution" were made under the leadership of the Chinese Communist Party, but it was also under the leadership of the Party that these mistakes were corrected. The personal experience of these mistakes brought home to the Chinese leaders that, on the one hand, China should not copy the Soviet model and, on the other, that they should take care to avoid other mistakes. These experiences were very valuable.

It should also be pointed out that China gained much positive experience apart from the lessons learned from these mistakes. For example, as early as 1956, Chen Yun(陈云), one of the Chinese leaders, proposed that in his vision of a socialist economy the state and collective economies would constitute the main body in the operation of industrial and commercial enterprises while an individual economy on a limited scale would be supplementary; planned production would constitute the main body in industrial and agricultural production, while free production determined by changes in the market and allowed within the framework of the state plan would be supplementary; and state markets would be the main body in a unified socialist market while free markets would be supplementary. Chen's opinions received great attention from the Party and the state leadership and played an important role in the economic readjustment of the early 1960s. Obviously this was an embryonic idea for the reform of the economic structure which broke away from the rigid Soviet model both in theory and in practice. Numerous reformist ideas such as this were put forward at that time by the Chinese leaders, cadres at different levels and professional researchers; some of them were put into practice to positive effect. Although these ideas were all drowned in the waves of the "cultural revolution", they heralded the reforms that began in 1978.

China initiated and implemented a policy of reform in 1978, two years after the end of the "cultural revolution". The reform of both the political and economic structure was carried out first in rural areas, and then extended to the cities and to various fields of industry, commerce and finance, etc. The reform has gone smoothly and achieved great successes in spite of the fact that some difficulties have been encountered. Through the reform we have found a socialist road suited to China's realities at the current stage which we call the socialist road with Chinese characteristics.

The current stage of socialism will continue into the first forty to fifty years of the next century. The economic structure that we have established and will further perfect has the following features: 1) A combination of economic planning with market regulation with the planned socialist market economy being vigorously developed; 2) An ownership structure based on socialist public ownership as the main body and the coexistence of multiple economic elements; and 3) a distribution system based on "giving to each according to his work" as the main form and supplemented by other forms of distribution. The purpose of economic structural reform and the correlative political structural reform is to bring into full play the initiative of the central and local authorities, enterprises, all social forces and the whole people, in order to promote economic development, make the country stronger and more powerful and bring about the common prosperity of the people.

Why has the reform in China proceeded more smoothly since 1978? Because reform actually began twenty years earlier and in the intervening years China accumulated rich experience and learned many lessons. In retrospect, we can see more clearly how important was the decision made by the Chinese leadership headed by Mao Zedong to break with the Soviet model in the 1950s. This decision led to an independent search for the correct road to socialist construction in China. The positive experiences of these twenty years have, of course, been very useful for the reform since 1978; the mistakes made in the course of research have also been of great value since they taught us a great deal and we learned things we had not known or not really known before.

From the late 1970s to the 1980s, the Chinese leaders with Deng Xiaoping (邓小平) as their representative conscientiously summarized both the positive and negative experiences of the past, and on this basis and proceeding from the nation's realities they proposed a full set of principles and policies related to China's reform, opening-up and the socialist road with Chinese characteristics. Past experiences also induced the Chinese people to be open-minded towards, and take an active part in, the reform.

Generally speaking, every social policy undergoes reform during the process of maturation. Reforms have been carried out in many capitalist countries within the framework of capitalism. The socialist system is also subject to change and therefore reform is a constant necessity. However, the reform I'm talking about has its own particular implication, that is, reform of the rigid economic structure with its over-concentration of power. The formation of this structure, as I have just said, was related not only to Soviet influence, but also to the historical conditions in a given period. Such a structure, if retained for a long period, inevitably leads a nation into a blind alley.

During the process of reform in China, care must be taken to prevent a recurrence of such mistakes as the Great Leap Forward and the "cultural revolution". Now that we know from past experience that reform is necessary and that we have found the correct road, there is no reason why we will stop or retreat.

I believe what I have said above is enough to explain why China must and can persevere with reform.

## III

I will now discuss the question of opening to the outside world.

One cannot talk about China's history of opening-up without saying a few words about modern China before 1949.

China was forced to open its doors to the outside world by the pressure of the gunboat policy of the imperialist powers. From the 1840s onwards, China was subjected on numerous occasions to foreign military aggression and a variety of unequal treaties were forced upon her. Foreigners enjoyed many privileges in China and were not subject to Chinese laws. They also controlled China's customs. They could freely establish banks, commercial houses and factories, and set up schools and churches according to their own rules. The imperialist powers also stationed their troops on China's soil. In the late Qing dynasty and the Republic of China period, the various administrations maintained their rule by ingratiating themselves with the imperialists and begging them for mercy. They followed the bidding of foreign powers when making important domestic and foreign decisions, while the imperialist powers, in their turn, supported the Chinese ruling groups in order to maintain their own privileges in China.

At that time, China was, so to speak, wide open, but at the cost of losing its sovereignty, i. e. , China was opened to and had intercourse with foreign countries not as an independent country, but as a semi-colonial nation. We cannot say that opening-up of this kind was absolutely unconducive to China's economic and cultural development, but in general it brought great suffering to the Chinese nation.

Although China's doors were nominally wide open at that time, they were not open in the true sense, either economically or culturally. The root cause was not a blockade but, to put it succinctly, poverty. The volume of China's foreign trade was minute. Being so poor and backward, how could the nation spare great quantities of products for export? Since the majority of the Chinese people, mostly peasants, were in rags and had insufficient food, how could China have large commodity markets? At that time few people could afford to go abroad, and most of the Chinese in foreign countries were those who could not make a living at home and had therefore gone abroad to do hard labor. Seen in this light, China was not open. It may well be said that foreign aggression forced China to open its doors with unequal terms, and at the same time that such aggression was the root cause of China's poverty and backwardness, which in turn prevented China from being truly open.

The conclusion drawn by the Chinese people from history was not that China should return to seclusion, refusing to open to the outside, but that the nation should first extricate itself from its semi-colonial status, that is, shake off imperialist control and oppression. Only after this had been accomplished would it be possible for China to have exchanges with other countries on an equal footing as an independent nation, shake off poverty and backwardness and acquire the conditions for opening-up in a normal way.

The People's Republic of China received support from people throughout the country as soon as it was established because they saw that this new regime had been born during the struggle against imperialism and would be able to defend China's independence and sovereignty.

Opening-up to the outside world has been practiced as one of China's basic policies since 1978. Does this mean that China had pursued a contrary policy for all of the previous thirty years?

I mentioned previously that Mao Zedong proposed learning from other countries in his speech in 1956. He explained that "Our policy is to learn from the strong points of all nations and all countries, learn all that is genuinely good in the political, economic, scientific and technological fields and in literature and art. But we must learn with an analytical and critical eye, not blindly, and we mustn't copy everything indiscriminately and transplant mechanically. Naturally, we mustn't pick up their shortcomings and weak points." He added that "We must firmly reject and criticize all the decadent bourgeois systems, ideologies and ways of life of foreign countries. But this should in no way prevent us from learning the advanced sciences and technologies of capitalist countries and whatever is scientific in the management of their enterprises. In the industrially developed countries they run their enterprises with few people and greater efficiency and they know how to do business. All this should be learned well in accordance with our own principles in order to improve our work." Naturally, China must be open to the outside world if it wanted to learn from all other countries.

As soon as New China was founded, the nation was ready to establish diplomatic relations with foreign countries on the basis of a mutual respect for sovereignty and territorial integrity, equality and mutual benefit, and to engage in normal trade and other economic contacts. However, as is well known, the government of the U-nited States adopted a policy of non-recognition towards the People's Republic of China. The United States launched the Korean War as a military threat against China, interfered with China's internal affairs on the question of Taiwan, enforced a blockade and placed an embargo on trade with China, obstructed the restoration of a seat in the United Nations to China, and did everything possible to exclude China from the international community. This policy of US government influenced many other countries. Under such conditions, China's desire to establish normal relations with all other nations, including the developed capitalist nations, could not be fulfilled and it was impossible for China to implement a policy of all-round opening-up.

China wishes to implement a policy of opening to the world, but there is a higher principle governing this policy; the maintenance of national independence and full sovereignty. The Chinese people, who have suffered enough during their history, value highly the principles of safeguarding their independence and keeping the initiative, and do their best to maintain national dignity. If the government of New China had abandoned these principles in her contacts with other countries, the people would have cast the government aside.

Although the Soviet leadership adopted a skeptical attitude towards the victory of the Chinese revolution in 1949, the Soviet Union was the only country that supported and gave aid to China on the basis of equality and mutual benefit. Therefore, as Mao Zedong said at that time, China had to "fall in one direction", that is, move to the socialist camp headed by the Soviet Union. However, in the 1960s when the Soviet Union waved its baton over the head of China, made demands that amounted to violation of China's independence and sovereignty, and tried to bring Chinese diplomacy within its global strategy, China resolutely resisted Soviet pressure and never yielded, firmly adhering to the principle that national independence and sovereignty are supreme.

When we say that the principle of independence is higher than the policy of opening-up we do not mean that the two are always in opposition and can never be reconciled. Under normal conditions they are compatible. China's experience over a long period of time has shown that opening to the outside world at the expense of national independence and sovereignty only allows the country to be exploited, and brings damage and humiliation, with the result that there is no genuine opening-up. The experience of many other countries also testifies to the fact that a nation can only implement a normal opening-up policy when it possesses full sovereignty and has developed its own economy.

In October 1970, the People's Republic of China's lawful seat in the United Nations was restored after various barriers had been overcome. In September 1972, China established diplomatic relations with Japan. In January 1979, diplomatic relations were established between China and the United States. Among the countries of Western Europe, the Scandinavian nations and France had established diplomatic ties with China in the 1950s and 1960s; Italy, Belgium, Britain, the Netherlands, the Federal Republic of Germany and Spain did the same in the 1970s. China also established official relations with the European Economic Community. China always enjoyed friendly relations with many countries in the third world, and such relations developed further from the 1970s onwards. These developments made it possible for China to initiate and carry out a policy of all-round opening-up.

The *Decision of the CPC Central Committee on Reform of the Economic Structure* adopted in 1984 said, "We must draw on the world's advanced methods of management, including those of developed capitalist countries, that conform to the laws of modern, socialized production." Another decision made in 1986 said, "We should do our utmost to learn from all countries (including the developed capitalist countries), to acquire advanced sciences and technologies, universally applicable expertise in economic management and administrative work and other useful knowledge and to verify and develop in practice what we have learned. " This is consistent with Mao Zedong's suggestion in 1956 that China should learn from foreign countries.

In the decade or so since 1978, while deepening its reform, China has also accelerated its opening to the outside world. Four cities in Guangdong and Fujian provinces and the whole province of Hainan were designated as special open economic zones. Fourteen coastal port cities became open cities, and the Yangtze River Delta, the Pearl River Delta and the delta area adjoining Xiamen, Quanzhou and Zhangzhou were designated coastal economic development areas. This formed a multi-level structure in terms of opening to the outside world, consisting of the special economic zones, the coastal open cities, the coastal economic development zones, and the hinterland regions. The Pudong Development Zone in Shanghai now under construction is another major step in making China's doors open even wider.

Coastal and hinterland areas, rural areas and cities throughout China's 9. 6 million square kilometers of territory have taken an active part in opening-up. The volume of both foreign trade imports and exports is increasing annually, and more and more foreign capital and advanced technology is being introduced. Economic, technological and cultural exchanges with overseas countries are expanding, and the number of Chinese students going abroad to study is increasing. Economic development in urban and rural areas has made it possible for China to open its doors wider, which in turn has boosted the nation's economic development.

In the world of today no country can develop in iso-

lation from others. Yet this alone is not enough to explain why China has adopted a policy of opening to the
outside world. China is a big country with a very large
population, if it does not rely on its own efforts and
bring its own potential into full play but relies on other
countries for everything, it will never achieve full development. However, China can strengthen its ability for
self-development by opening to the outside world. China
has built socialism on a weak economic foundation, but
the consolidation of socialism must rely on tremendous
economic development that can only be achieved by em-
ploying modern science and technology, and which must
be based on large-scale socialized production. Therefore,
we must excel at absorbing the useful achievements of
mankind in our socialist construction, which is of special
importance to China. This is the basic reason why China
has stressed from the very beginning learning from other
nations in its socialist production, and why China must
implement its policy of opening to the outside world.

China's opening to the outside world is based on the
principle of equality and mutual benefit. Foreign trade
and the introduction of foreign capital are conducted in
the belief that they are beneficial to the foreign side as
well as to China. Gone forever are the days when according to the unequal treaties China opened its doors at
the expense of its sovereignty. It is a fantasy to think
that now China needs to open to the outside world new
unequal treaties detrimental to China's independence and
sovereign integrity can be imposed. On the other hand,
no foreign forces can isolate China and make things so
difficult for her that the nation must abandon her policy
of opening up to the outside world.

From what has been said above one can see clearly

why China will persist in carrying out its policy of opening to the outside world.

## IV

Finally, I wish to conclude my speech with the following lines.

Some people say that reform and opening to the outside world will divert China onto the capitalist road. This is a misunderstanding.

China has held to the socialist road and at the same time persevered in reform and opening-up since 1978. I have said that China's socialist road was not decided by the subjective will of a few people. Objective historical conditions determined that only by taking the socialist road could China hope to develop and prosper. What I have said previously shows socialism is not incompatible with reform and opening to the outside world. Reform is the self-perfection of socialism and the aim of reform is to find a socialist road suited to the specific conditions in China. China's opening-up is a basic element of the reform and is carried out on the basis of socialism. Socialism has ensured independence and the beginning of prosperity for China, which in turn have made normal opening-up possible. Opening to the outside world has in its turn accelerated socialist development. Although on the way forward there will be many problems to solve and many difficulties to overcome, China will not, and cannot, give up the policy of reform and opening-up or deviate from the socialist road.

With a tragic history that lasted for one hundred years, the Chinese people will never again allow their country to be torn apart, to be trampled once again by foreign powers, or again beg for a living. If it deviated from the socialist road, China would disintegrate and there would be violent social upheavals, causing the stagnation of economic development and reducing China to a source of contention among the world powers. At the same time China would become a burden for the world. If that happened, it would be a disaster not only for the Chinese people, but for the world.

Today China has social stability and concentrates on economic development under the socialist system; at the same time the nation is attempting to perfect and further consolidate this system through reform and opening-up in order to bring prosperity to the state and the people. In this way China will become a positive factor in the common development of all countries of the world and a powerful force for defending world peace.

> (Delivered on 13 November 1991 and first
> published in *Seeking Truth*, 1992, no. 5,
> 1 March)

# Two Major Undertakings by Mao Zedong During His Lifetime

## —To Commemorate the Centenary of Mao Zedong's Birth

Mao Zedong always attached great importance to the October Revolution in Russia, the influence of the existence of the Soviet Union on the Chinese revolution, and the experience of the October Revolution and socialist construction in the Soviet Union. The following is a very well-known remark made by Comrade Mao Zedong in 1949: "The salvoes of the October Revolution brought us Marxism-Leninism. The October Revolution helped progressives in China, as throughout the world, to adopt the proletarian world outlook as the instrument for studying a nation's destiny and considering anew their own problems. Follow the path of the Russians — that was their conclusion."[1]

While cherishing a high regard for the experiences of the October Revolution and the Soviet socialist construction, Mao Zedong firmly opposed the imposition of the model of the October Revolution on the Chinese revolution, and did not bow to the baton waved over the heads of the Chinese people by the leaders of the Soviet

[1] Mao Zedong, *Selected Works*, Beijing, Foreign Languages Press, 1977, Vol. IV, p. 413

Union (and the Communist International) based on their experience and in their own interests.

The Chinese Communist Party blazed a new path for the Chinese revolution and won the final victory. Now we are following a road with Chinese characteristics in our socialist construction. If China had not rejected the baton of the Soviet leaders (and also that of the Communist International, or of the Soviet leaders through the Communist International) and taken the Soviet model of revolution and construction as the only possible course, it would not have found its own road.

It was because Mao Zedong attached importance to the experience of the Soviet revolution and construction, but at the same time did not have blind faith in it and waged a resolute struggle against such blind faith, that he became a great leader who creatively found the correct road for democratic revolution in China and led the revolution to victory. Furthermore, he was also the first to propose the search for a road with Chinese characteristics in socialist construction.

In 1942, Mao Zedong launched a rectification movement（整风运动）within the Party to combat subjectivism and, in particular, dogmatism. To counter the dogmatist tendency predominant within the Party, Mao Zedong pointed out that we should by no means regard odd quotations from Marx, Engels, Lenin and Stalin as dogma, but must apply the Marxist-Leninist stand, viewpoint and method to the study of present conditions and the history of China, and make concrete analysis of and find solution to the problems of the Chinese revolution. This movement was, of course, meant for the Party organizations in China, but his criticism of a dogmatism divorced from China's realities had wider implications. In the 1930s, the dogmatists within the Communist Party of China (CPC) accepted opinions from Moscow as if they were infallible laws that had to be obeyed, no matter how much they ran counter to China's realities. Like their masters, they also took isolated sentences from Marx, Engels, Lenin and Stalin as dogma.

In 1938, Mao Zedong emphatically pointed out before the movement to rectify the Party's work style that the Chinese Communist Party must "learn to apply the theory of Marxism-Leninism to the specific circumstances of China. " He also said, "For the Chinese Communists who are part of the great Chinese nation, flesh of its flesh and blood of its blood, any talk about Marxism in isolation from China's characteristics is merely Marxism in the abstract, Marxism in a vacuum. Hence to apply Marxism concretely in China so that its every manifestation has an indubitably Chinese character, i. e. , to apply Marxism in the light of China's specific characteristics, becomes a problem which it is urgent for the whole Party to understand and solve. "[1]

China, of course, had much in common with other countries in its revolution, and in this respect the Soviet Union and the Communist International gave valuable assistance to the Chinese Communists, mainly at the time when the Communist Party of China was born and in its infancy. At that time, the Chinese Communists were totally inexperienced and knew very little about Marxist theory. As in other colonies and dependencies, the revolution in China was not yet a proletarian social-

---

[1] *Ibid.*, Vol. II, p. 209.

ist revolution, but a bourgeois democratic revolution. The Chinese Communists had an understanding of the proletarian socialist revolution from the Soviet Union and the Communist International. Such an understanding was very important, but the general theory could not be taken as a guide to the revolution in China if it was not combined with Chinese realities. It is true that the reasons for the utter defeat of the Chinese revolution in 1927 were the great disparity in strength between the revolutionary and the counter-revolutionary forces, and the lack of independent judgment on the part of the Chinese Communists, but the defeat was also the fault of the leaders of the Soviet Union and the Communist International, who were far from China and issued orders for the Chinese revolution purely on the strength of abstract concepts. Their representatives occupied leading position, yet the more complicated the situation became, the more arbitrary and impractical were their directions, because they did not have a clear understanding of the actual conditions in China.

In the first half of the 1930s, the Communist International and its officials issued arbitrary and impractical directions for the revolution in China and caused extremely serious damage. By this time the Chinese communists had gained some experience of their own and, with Mao Zedong as their representative, they established a number of rural revolutionary bases with unique Chinese features. However, for a number of complex reasons, the Chinese Communist Party was unable to resist the baton charges from Moscow. Under the direction of an official from the Far Eastern Bureau of the Communist International, a few inexperienced young students who had returned from the Soviet Union, led by Wang Ming (Chen Shaoyu), controlled the central leadership of the Party. On the orders of their masters, they pursued a "Left" line, regardless of China's national conditions. Militarily, they denounced the strategies and tactics that had been formulated by Mao Zedong and other comrades and which had proved effective, and handed over the right to command the Red Army on a silver platter to foreign officers sent to China by the Communist International, whose only experience was of the First World War. As a result, the impressive achievements of the Chinese communists in their arduous struggle following the disastrous defeat in 1927 (including the revolutionary bases built by the Red Army and the work in the White Areas) were almost completely negated.

If the Chinese communists headed by Mao Zedong had not corrected the "Left" line and changed the Party's leadership at the January 1935 meeting in Zunyi and thus turned the tide, there would not have been the victory of the Long March and the Chinese revolution would not have been extricated from a critical predicament. The Zunyi meeting was an epoch-making symbol of the fact that the Chinese communists had begun to deal independently with the problems encountered in the revolution in their own country.

In 1938, after the War of Resistance Against Japan had broken out, the Chinese revolution was harassed once more by the Communist International. Wang Ming, who held an important post in the leading body of the Communist International, was sent back to China. He brought with him a number of ideas and measures designed to make the Party's policies with regard to the anti-Japanese united front turn to the right. Since he had the backing of the Soviet Union and the Communist International, it was only with great difficulty that the Party managed to overcome the influence of his erroneous thinking. The whole process of the War of Resistance Against Japan proved that it was absolutely necessary and possible to establish a united front with the Kuomintang. However, the Party had to adhere firmly to the principle of independence, using its own initiative within the united front, and carry out a strategy of both unity and struggle, that is, seeking unity through struggle. Only in this way could the united front be maintained right up to the final victory in the war.

If we had abandoned struggle and begged for unity the united front would certainly have failed. Wang Ming failed in his attempt to pursue the Rightist line within the Party, but the leaders of the Soviet Union and the Communist International showed no appreciation for any of the strategies adopted by the Chinese Communist Party with Mao Zedong as its leader, and were even suspicious of them.

As a result of the differences between the social and historical conditions in China and those in Western countries, new factors not mentioned in Marxist texts were bound to crop up during the Chinese revolution. The most striking of these was that the vanguard of the proletariat went to the economically backward countryside to arouse the masses and build up the revolutionary armed forces. Beginning with the concrete historical and social conditions in China, and based on the experience of China's revolutionary struggle, Mao Zedong formulated the concept of building rural revolutionary bases and discovered the correct road of encircling the cities from the countryside. He thus developed Marxism with these new viewpoints and ideas. Without great theoretical courage, he would never have proposed and insisted upon these viewpoints and ideas. Generally speaking, people have to smash the bonds of tradition before they propose new viewpoints and ideas, so they must have theoretical courage. At that time, it was none other than the leaders of the Communist International and the Soviet Communist Party, the universally acknowledged authorities on interpreting Marxism, who took Marxist propositions as dogma and turned them into conventions that would shackle the minds of the people. It was extremely difficult for anyone to shake off the yoke.

In his speech on the rectification of the work style of the Party, Mao Zedong only touched on problems within the Chinese Communist Party and nothing else, but the leaders of the Soviet Union and the Communist International viewed the rectification movement initiated by Mao in the early 1940s as heresy. There were two possible reasons for this: Firstly, Wang Ming, the favorite of the Soviet Union and the Communist International, was the main target of the rectification movement; secondly, the leaders of the Soviet Union and the Communist International had in their minds ready-made formulas that rigidly followed the Marxist texts and were based on the Russian experience. For example, they believed that any revolution led by the proletariat should take the cities as its base, and China was no exception. However, the rectification launched by Mao Zedong actually challenged and negated this formula.

Mao Zedong's speech *Rectify the Party's Style of Work*（改造我们的学习）, delivered in May 1941, was the first document to elucidate the basic concept of the rectification movement. In this speech, he incisively criticized the people inside the Party "who cannot open their mouths without citing ancient Greece. " They "chop up history, know only ancient Greece but not China. . . . "[1]"Ancient Greece" here might refer to the Soviet Union. It is true that Mao Zedong spoke highly of the *History of the Communists of the Soviet Union (Bolsheviks), A Short Course* written under the direction of Stalin (whether this appraisal is correct or not is open to reconsideration), but he put it this way, "When we see how Lenin and Stalin integrated the universal truth of Marxism with the concrete practice of the Soviet revolution and thereby developed Marxism, we shall know how we should work in China. "[2] It can thus be seen that Mao did not consider the Soviet experience universally applicable, and he stressed the integration of the universal truth of Marxism with the concrete practice of the Chinese revolution.

Comrade Deng Xiaoping said, "The Chinese revolution was carried out not by adopting the model of the Russian October Revolution but by proceeding from the realities in China, by using the rural areas to encircle the cities and seize power with armed force. "[3] If the Chinese revolution had deviated from the road that conformed to China's national conditions and followed the track the foreign authorities took for granted, there would not have been the protracted war against Japan nor victory in 1949.

The Communist International was disbanded in

---

[1] *Ibid*.,Vol. III, pp. 19—21.

[2] *Ibid*., p. 24.

[3] Deng Xiaoping, *Selected Works* (1975—1982), Beijing, Foreign Languages Press, 1984, p. 300.

June 1943, but during the years immediately before its dissolution, its interference with the Communist Party of China became less and less. Comrade Zhou Enlai said, "The Chinese Communist Party had grown more mature by that time and had fewer dealings with the Communist International. "[1]

During the War of Resistance Against Japan, the Soviet leadership was skeptical, to say the least, about what the armed forces led by the Communist Party of China were doing. They could not fully understand the significance of the guerrilla warfare in rural areas or the strategy of encircling the cities from the countryside. Neither could they understand the dual tactics of both unity and struggle within the united front. During the time of the War of Liberation, Soviet leaders did not believe that the Chinese revolution could win a complete victory, nor did they think it advisable that the Chinese revolution should win a complete victory. This was partly the result of their mistaken assessment of the world situation and their inability to understand the unique strategy adopted during the Chinese revolution of encircling the cities from the countryside.

Mao Zedong was of the opinion that Stalin's mistakes amounted to only 30 per cent of the whole and his achievements 70 per cent. He said: "Stalin did a number of wrong things in connection with China. The 'Left' adventurism pursued by Wang Ming in the latter part of the Second Revolutionary Civil War period and his Right opportunism in the early days of the War of Resistance Against Japan can both be traced to Stalin. At the time

---

[1] Zhou Enlai, *Selected Works*, Beijing, Renmin Press, 1981, Vol. II, p. 312.

of the War of Liberation, Stalin first enjoined us not to press on with the revolution, maintaining that if civil war flared up, the Chinese nation would run the risk of destroying itself. Then when fighting did erupt, he took us half seriously, half skeptically. When we won the war, Stalin suspected that ours was a victory of the Tito type, and in 1949 and 1950 the pressure on us was very strong indeed. "[1]

Zhou Enlai once commented that Stalin was sometimes skeptical about the Communist party of China, but that he had changed his opinion once his skepticism proved groundless. "For example, he suspected we were sham Marxists, reconciling with imperialism, but the War of Resisting U. S. Aggression and Aiding Korea changed his opinion. "[2]

All of this shows that Stalin viewed the Communist Party of China with great suspicion until the victory of the Chinese revolution in 1949. Such suspicion was concentrated on Mao Zedong, the most creative leader in theoretical terms in the Communist Party of China. Deng Xiaoping said, "During the period when Stalin was in power, the Chinese Communist Party did not follow his advice in dealing with certain crucial questions, and because it did not, it led the revolution to victory. "[3] The Chinese Communist Party was able to proceed from the realities and withstand pressure from outside; this was due mainly to Mao Zedong.

Deng Xiaoping appropriately pointed out, "Chair-

---

[1] Mao Zedong, *op. cit.*, Vol. V, p. 304.

[2] Zhou Enlai, *op. cit.*, Vol. II, p. 302.

[3] Deng Xiaoping, *Selected Works*, Beijing, Renmin Press, 1993 & 1994, Vol. III, p. 37.

man Mao's greatest contribution was that he applied the principles of Marxism-Leninism to the concrete practice of the Chinese revolution, pointing the way to victory."[1] This contribution cannot be overestimated. Therefore Comrade Deng Xiaoping said, "Without him the Chinese people would, at the very least, have spent much more time groping in the dark."[2]

China had basically completed its socialist transformation by 1956, and had begun to face the problem of how to proceed with socialist construction. In 1953 China had begun the first Five Year Plan, while also carrying out the socialist transformation of agriculture and capitalist industry and commerce. Both the methods and policies adopted during the transformation conformed to national conditions and had Chinese characteristics. This was an entirely new undertaking, but the experience we acquired both in organizing the peasants after they had gained land from the landlords and in uniting the national capitalists in the period of democratic revolution helped us find a way for socialist transformation suited to Chinese national conditions. Economic construction during the First Five Year Plan period was carried out mainly on the basis of the Soviet experience, since the Chinese Communist Party had only limited experience in the economic development of the rural revolutionary bases, which was obviously not enough, and little useful experience had been handed down from old China.

In a speech *On the Ten Major Relationships* made in April 1956,[3] Mao Zedong said: "In the Soviet Union

---

[1]  Deng Xiaoping, *Selected Works* (1975—1982), p. 345.

[2]  *Ibid.*, p. 326.

[3]  Mao Zedong, *op. cit.*, Vol. V, p. 284—307.

certain defects and errors that occurred in the course of their building socialism have lately come to light. Do you want the detours they have made? It was by drawing lessons from their experience that we were able to avoid certain detours in the past, and there is all the more reason for us to do so now. " The statement that "we were able to avoid certain detours in the past" might refer to the victories during the period of socialist transformation, but perhaps also includes the victories during the period of the democratic revolution. What lessons should China draw from the Soviet Union in the course of socialist construction? In what respects should China be different? Mao Zedong mentioned the following specific points in this regard:

Firstly, they lop-sidedly "stress on heavy industry to the neglect of agriculture and light industry . . . . "

Secondly, "The Soviet Union has adopted measures which squeeze the peasants very hard. It takes away too much from the peasants at too low a price through its system of so-called obligatory sales and other measures. " "In view of the grave mistakes made by the Soviet Union on this question, we must take greater care and handle the relationship between the state and the peasants well. "

Thirdly, "We must not follow the example of the Soviet Union in concentrating everything in the hands of the central authorities, shackling the local authorities and denying them the right to independent action. " He also said in this speech that "it's not right, I'm afraid, to place everything in the hands of the central or the provincial and municipal authorities without leaving the factories any power of their own, any room for independent action, any benefits. "

Fourthly, "In the Soviet Union the relationship between the Russian nationality and the minority nationalities is very abnormal; we should draw lessons from this."

Fifthly, "Which is better, to have just one party or several? As we see it now, it's perhaps better to have several parties. This has been true in the past and may well be so for the future; it means long-term coexistence and mutual supervision." "In this respect, China is different from the Soviet Union."

Sixthly, "In those days when the dogmatists headed by Wang Ming were in the saddle, our Party erred on this question [i. e. , the question of how to deal with people who have made mistakes], picking up the bad aspect of Stalin's style of work. In society the dogmatists rejected the middle forces and inside the Party they did not allow people to correct their mistakes; they barred both from the revolution." "They barred from the revolution those who had committed errors, drawing no distinction between the making of mistakes and counter-revolution, and went so far as to kill a number of people who were guilty of only mistakes." With regard to this question, Mao Zedong, Zhou Enlai and others constantly exhorted the Party not to set up a "security" organization with a vertical chain of command from the top down to the grass roots level and divorced from the Party leadership.

Seventhly, "We have put forward the slogan of learning from other countries. I think we have been right. At present the leaders of some countries are chary and even afraid of advancing this slogan." It is obvious here to which countries the "some countries" refers. Mao continued: "We must firmly reject and criticize all the decadent bourgeois systems, ideologies and ways of life of foreign countries. But this should in no way prevent us from learning the advanced sciences and technologies of capitalist countries and whatever is scientific in the management of their enterprises. "

In this speech Mao Zedong raised ten topics, i. e. , ten major relationships. He said: "It is to focus on one basic policy that these ten problems are being raised, the basic policy of mobilizing all positive factors, internal and external, to serve the cause of socialism. " This basic policy was formulated on the basis of lessons learnt from the Soviet Union. By this time, Mao Zedong had already seen that the economic and political structure, with an over-concentration of power, everything organized under state plans, and a tendency to separate the socialist economy from the rest of the world, were not helpful for mobilizing all positive factors at home and abroad and therefore not desirable. Mao Zedong believed that China could, and should, find a way to build socialism that corresponded to China's specific conditions and which was different from that in the Soviet Union. Such an opinion was shocking and incredible, since both at the time and later the Soviet model was accepted by the Soviet leadership and theoreticians as the only conceivable option. Almost everyone in the world, whether they opposed or supported socialism, thought likewise. Those opposed to socialism regarded the drawbacks of the Soviet model as inherent in Marxism and socialism, while those in favor of socialism generally believed one must copy the Soviet model to construct socialism.

This demonstrates that the Chinese communists were aware of the shortcomings and mistakes and, in order to avoid them, tried to blaze their own trail which accorded with China's concrete conditions. However, this does not mean that they found such a path. In the process of the democratic revolution, the Communist Party of China travelled a long and tortuous road and suffered numerous setbacks and defeats. It was only after summing up its experience and lessons, especially those learnt from its setbacks and defeats, that the Party found its own path to victory. It could not have been otherwise in the process of socialist construction.

In *On the Ten Major Relationships* Mao Zedong stated that factories and every unit of production must enjoy independence as the correlative of centralization if they were to develop more vigorously. He also said, "... our attention should now be focussed on how to enlarge the powers of the local authorities to some extent, give them greater independence and let them do more, all on the premise that the united leadership of the central authorities is to be strengthened." These were new ideas in an embryonic form that tended to break through the Soviet model. Other leaders of the Chinese Communist Party also had their own new ideas. For instance, Comrade Chen Yun proposed "three main bodies" and "three supplements" (i. e. , the state and collective economies, planned production and state markets as the main bodies, supplemented by the individual economy, free production and free markets). [1] However, these ideas in their embryonic form had to be put into practice before they could develop into a new structure and replace the old one.

---

[1]  Chen Yun, *Selected Works* (1956 — 1958), Beijing, Renmin Press, 1986, p. 13.

In 1980, Comrade Deng Xiaoping granted an interview to an Italian correspondent who touched on the question of whether Mao Zedong made any mistakes. He asked: "Wasn't the 'Great Leap Forward' a mistake? Wasn't copying the Soviet model a mistake?" Deng Xiaoping made an incisive reply without referring specifically to the question of "copying the Soviet model." The socialist construction in China was indeed heavily influenced by the Soviet model, but Mao Zedong was the leader who most vehemently opposed copying the Soviet model. Under the leadership of Mao Zedong, the Chinese Communist Party repudiated the "unalterable principles" affirmed by the Soviet leaders and, proceeding from China's national conditions, found their own path during the period of democratic revolution. As a result of experience Mao Zedong was convinced that the Chinese Communist Party should also forge a new path in socialist construction. As a matter of fact, he was mistaken in the "Great Leap Forward" and the people's communes and, finally, he made a great mistake in the "cultural revolution", but he did not make the mistake of copying the Soviet model. On the contrary, he did his best to break away from the Soviet model and, in search of a new path that suited China, took the wrong track. It was because he took the wrong track that he found no correct solution and China could not cast off the yoke of the Soviet model.

In *On the Ten Major Relationships* Mao Zedong said, "In the past we followed this policy of mobilizing all positive factors in order to put an end to the rule of imperialism, feudalism and bureaucrat-capitalism and to win victory for the people's democratic revolution. We are now following the same policy in order to carry on the socialist revolution and build a socialist country. " This remark is correct, but we should differentiate construction from revolution when making use of the experience gained from the past. The methods for bringing all positive factors into play during the period of construction could not be the same as in the previous period of revolution. If we applied the experience gained during the period of democratic revolution uncritically to the socialist construction, we would inevitably make mistakes.

In the period of democratic revolution we made full use of the concept of class struggle, which was closely linked to the broad masses and aroused their political enthusiasm, so producing inexhaustible forces to oppose the enemy. However, this experience should not be used in a simplified manner in socialist construction. Mobilizing the masses using only political means and "taking class struggle as the key link" resulted in gross mistakes such as broadening the scope of the anti-Rightist struggle, the "Great Leap Forward", the people's communes and, finally, the "cultural revolution," which led us astray in our socialist construction and caused enormous losses.

As in the period of democratic revolution, the Chinese communists were taught profound lessons by mistakes made during the period of socialist construction. In 1976, after the end of the "cultural revolution," the Chinese communists led by Deng Xiaoping summarized the experiences of the past twenty years at the Third Plenary Session of the Eleventh Central Committee of the Chinese Communist Party, especially the "Left" errors that led to the dangerous "cultural revolution," and then corrected these mistakes. At last they were clear about the real national conditions in China, and that the nation was still at the primary stage of socialism. They adopted a series of general and specific policies centered around "one central task, two basic points" (the central task is economic development; the two basic points are adherence to the Four Cardinal Principles and implementation of reform and the open policy).

Reviewing the twenty years of tortuous development of socialist construction from 1957 onwards, we can see that the numerous mistakes made were not the result of copying the Soviet model, but resulted from endeavors to make a fresh start and adopting another policy line. When examining the history of this period, can we conclude that we should not have doubted the Soviet model and that had we copied the Soviet model we could have avoided such mistakes? I believe that any such conclusion would be absolutely wrong.

There were two paths open to China in 1956; one was the path actually followed for the subsequent twenty or so years; the other was to follow the example of the Soviet Union. The Soviet leaders at least thought that China should take the latter course. What would have happened if we had taken that road? China would not only have taken an unsound socialist road, but would also have become a "satellite" of the Soviet U-nion. Although copying the Soviet model was different from becoming a "satellite," the two were closely related. History shows that during the Stalinist era the Soviet Union was used to waving its baton at will in the international communist movement. Stalin's successors did not analyze his rights and wrongs scientifically; although they totally denounced him they continued in his erroneous style. They continued to see the Soviet Communist Party as a patriarchal party and adopted a great-nation chauvinist attitude towards other socialist states. It was only because of firm resistance from the leadership of the Chinese Communist Party headed by Mao Zedong that China was not reduced to a "satellite" of the Soviet Union.

Despite objections from the Soviet Union, from the late 1950s onwards, Mao Zedong continued to explore China's own socialist road, and at the same time vigilantly watched the increasing hostility of the Soviet leaders towards China. Nikita Khrushchev threatened to drive China out of the socialist camp and made direct demands on China that amounted to violation of China's sovereignty and control of China's destiny, to which the whole Communist Party of China gave an uncompromising reply. I will not go into the details of the heated debate between the two parties in the early 1960s. While it must be admitted that some of the arguments put forward by the Chinese side were not entirely correct, it was absolutely right for the Communist Party of China to defend state sovereignty and the right of any socialist country to follow its own road according to its own national conditions. Perhaps China was not exaggerating when the Soviet Union was said to be practicing socialist imperialism, since the Soviet Union resorted to everything, including armed force, to maintain its authority. Since Nikita Khrushchev and his successor Leonid Brezhnev held on to their socialist imperialism, while on the other side Mao Zedong and his comrades were determined to preserve the independence of their party and the sovereignty of their state, the split between the Chinese and the Soviet parties was inevitable and lasted for a long time.

In the early 1960s, after careful consideration, Mao Zedong made the decision to defend China's independence and sovereignty at the cost of breaking with the Soviet Union. This was a very difficult decision that could have led to aggression from the north and, at the same time, to China's complete isolation from the rest of the world, because at that time the Soviet Union was a great military power and wielded a rather effective baton in the international communist movement. In China itself, it was not easy to change the people's long-standing reverence for the Soviet Union. Mao Zedong encountered many difficult and complex situations during his life which required that he make the correct decisions. This particular decision had far-reaching historical significance and displayed to the full his ability to solve the knottiest problems.

Even if there were those who doubted the correctness and necessity of this decision before 1989, after the radical social changes that took place in eastern Europe and the Soviet Union between 1989 and 1991, no one now underestimates the importance of Mao Zedong's decision made thirty years ago. If Mao Zedong had not made such a decision and China had taken the second path and become a Soviet "satellite," what would China be like today? Perhaps many people discussing this issue would reach the same conclusion. The normalization of Sino-Soviet relations shortly before the disintegration of the Soviet Union was also absolutely necessary, since the situation was no longer the same as thirty years previously, and such normalization laid the foundation for the current friendly relations between China and the various states of the former Soviet Union.

Once China chose the first road, many detours and

mistakes were made in its exploration; in the "cultural revolution" the fate of the party and the state hung in the balance. It is now useless to feel dejected at these detours and mistakes, and it is meaningless to say that since both roads were equally undesirable it would have been better for us to take the road we are now following in 1957 rather than as late as 1978. As a matter of fact, it was as a result of experiencing these detours and mistakes that the correct path appropriate for China was found in 1978 after the Third Plenary Session of the Eleventh Central Committee of the Chinese Communist Party. The party was able to do this because it has a tradition of learning from past mistakes. The formation of this tradition was closely linked to Mao Zedong, who, in the period of democratic revolution, learnt from the numerous mistakes made by the party and adopted the doctrines and policies that led China's revolution to victory. In the period of socialist construction, he also became aware of the shortcomings of the "Great Leap Forward" and the people's communes, and tried to correct them. However, because he lacked a thorough understanding of these mistakes, he did not take any effective measures. In the later period of the "cultural revolution," which he himself launched, he began to realize that at the least this so-called revolution fell short of what he had hoped for. However, it was too late for him to learn from the experience and he had to leave it to the next generation.

The new leadership of the Communist Party of China established at the Third Plenary Session of the Eleventh Central Committee both corrected the mistakes made by Mao Zedong in his later years and continued his correct line of thought. How could such a leadership emerge so soon after the "cultural revolution?" As a matter of fact, this new generation of leaders was trained and raised by Mao Zedong himself. They grew up with and were tempered by the revolutionary practices guided by Mao Zedong thought, which combined the universal truth of Marxism-Leninism and China's concrete conditions. Deng Xiaoping, their outstanding representative, was one of the members of the leading group with Mao Zedong at the core.

Deng Xiaoping's theory of building socialism with Chinese characteristics is an inheritance from and development of Mao Zedong thought. In the decade or so since 1978, Mao Zedong's desire with regard to socialist construction in China has gradually become a reality. His desire was that China would be able to build socialism more quickly and with better results in a way appropriate to China's conditions, while avoiding the shortcomings and mistakes made in socialist construction in the Soviet Union. He also believed that in constructing socialism it was better to bring all positive factors into full play rather than have the initiative come from the state alone. Internationally, we should also do our best to mobilize all positive factors, both direct and indirect. Chinese communists finally discovered in the 1980s that a combination of reform, opening up, and a socialist market economy is the only correct way to bring every positive factor into play.

There was a rumor in China about a speech said to have been made by Mao Zedong on 13 June 1976, a few months before he passed away, when the "cultural revolution" seemed to be drawing to an end but nobody was sure how the situation would develop. In this speech

Mao Zedong reviewed his life and spoke of arrangements after his death. He said, inter alia, "There is a Chinese idiom: A final judgment can be passed on a person only when the lid is laid on his coffin. The lid has not been laid on my coffin yet, but very soon, so I think a final judgment can be passed on me now. " "I have done two things in my life. " The first thing he spoke of was the victory of the democratic revolution and the establishment of political power in China. He remarked, "Very few people raised an objection to this. A few people have chirped at my ears urging me to have a quick recovery of that island [Taiwan]— that's all there is to it. " "The other thing, as you know it, is the great cultural revolution. To this few people give their support and many raise an objection. "

It seems that Chairman Mao indeed made a speech to that effect to a few people from his sickbed. The notes might not be one hundred percent accurate but could not be far out either.

Mao Zedong was obviously not so confident about the "cultural revolution" at that time. However, his assessment was far removed from the historical conclusion. The conclusion with regard to the first topic that he mentioned is that it was a great victory which changed China's tragic lot and benefitted future generations, while the conclusion with regard to the second is that it was a great mistake and a defeat.

It is understandable that Mao Zedong considered the "cultural revolution" as one the two things he had done during his life, for it was indeed clearly stamped with his personal seal. However, when a general survey is made of Mao's whole life, later generations will not accept that the latter half of his life should be summarized as the great mistake of the "cultural revolution."

Mao Zedong fully succeeded in his search for the correct road for the Chinese democratic revolution in the first half of his life, but failed to reach his goal of finding the correct road for building socialism for China in the latter half of his life. Although in the process of exploration he made many detours and the gross mistake of the "cultural revolution," his initiative in making such explorations will go down in history.

In conclusion, Mao Zedong indeed had two major undertakings in his lifetime:

The first was that under his leadership the party and the people overthrew the rule of imperialism, feudalism, and bureaucrat capitalism in China and achieved a democratic revolution. Given China's actual conditions, in order to defeat their powerful enemies and achieve victory for the revolution, they could not copy the model of other countries but had to combine universal truth with the actual situation in China and blaze a new trail of their own. Mao Zedong dared to resist pernicious influences from outside, and both discovered and insisted on taking the road that could lead the Chinese revolution to victory. The first undertaking was thus a perfect success.

The second was that, after the socialist transformation with Chinese characteristics, he searched for China's own path towards socialist construction. Mao Zedong was the pioneer in this search. He led the whole party and people throughout the country in resisting strong influences and pressures, and persisted in this exploration. Mao Zedong should go down in history as a great pioneer. He did not live to see with his own eyes the positive results of this exploration, however, in his students' generation, his endeavors are blooming and bearing fruit.

(First published in *People's Daily*, 17 December, 1993)

## Appendix

### Notes on "Two Major Undertakings by Mao Zedong During His Lifetime"[1]

I presented a paper at this seminar entitled "Two Major Undertakings by Mao Zedong During His Lifetime," which was subsequently published in the 17 December edition of *People's Daily*. The paper is rather long, so I will not read it now. I think that you have perhaps already read this article and I hope you will oblige me with your valuable comments. I should now like to make the following comments in response to questions raised after my paper was published.

Firstly, in this article I quoted a remark by Deng Xiaoping on Chairman Mao: "Without him the Chinese people would, at the very least, have spent much more time groping in the dark."[2] A fuller quotation is as follows: "For most of his life, Chairman Mao did very good things. Many times he saved the Party and the state from crises. Without him the Chinese people would, at the very least, have spent much more time groping in the dark." Deng Xiaoping made this remark

---

[1] This speech was delivered by the author at the opening of the *Seminar on the Life and Thought of Mao Zedong* held on 26 December 1993. It was originally published in *Research on the History of the CPC*, 1994, no. 2 (published on 25 March). The two points that should be corrected mentioned in the fifth and seventh items in this article have already been corrected in "Two Major Undertakings by Mao Zedong During His Lifetime" in this book.

[2] Deng Xiaoping, *Selected Works (1975-1982)*, Beijing, Foreign Languages Press, 1984, p. 326.

in 1980.

Two years earlier, in December 1978, when he made a speech at the closing session of the Central Working Conference which made preparations for the Third Plenary Session of the Eleventh Central Committee of the Chinese Communist Party that immediately followed, Deng Xiaoping said, "If we look back at the years following the failure of the revolution in 1927, it appears very likely that without his outstanding leadership the Chinese revolution would still not have triumphed even today. In that case, the people of all our nationalities would still be suffering under the reactionary rule of imperialism, feudalism and bureaucrat-capitalism, and our Party would still be engaged in bitter struggle in the dark. Therefore, it is no exaggeration to say that were it not for Chairman Mao there would be no New China."[1]

These two remarks by Deng Xiaoping triggered off the following questions from some comrades: Was the victory of the Chinese revolution a historical necessity? If it was, what was the relationship between this victory and individual leaders?

In my view, the victory of the Chinese revolution certainly had a solid foundation, or a historical necessity. However, human society develops quite differently from nature. The latter develops spontaneously according to the necessity of objective realities (when there is no human intervention, of course), but is subject to interference from random factors, while the development of human society is brought about by the ideas and actions of human beings. Chairman Mao said in his famous

---

[1] *Ibid.*, p. 160

*On Protracted War*（论持久战），"Whatever is done has to be done by human beings; protracted war and final victory will not come about without human action." The victory of the Chinese revolution was, generally speaking, a historical necessity, but neither the form, thoroughness nor time of victory could be said to have been determined by historical necessity. Man's endeavors and actions, and the actions of revolutionary groups and their leaders certainly had a great bearing on the victory.

The Chinese revolution could be said to have been completely victorious, a complete victory against imperialism, feudalism and bureaucratic capitalism, and a victory of the new democratic revolution led by the proletariat. Chairman Mao said in *On New Democracy*（新民主主义论）that after the Russian October Revolution all the revolutionary struggles of oppressed peoples in colonies and semi-colonies had become part of the proletarian-socialist world revolution, and comprised a new democratic revolution led by the proletariat. However, judging by historical events since the Second World War, this statement is not quite accurate. The fact that the victory of the Chinese revolution was complete and a victory for the new democratic revolution could not be said to be historical destiny, but had a lot to do with the thinking of its leaders. This is even more the case with the time of victory. It can hardly be said that history decided that China would win its revolution in 1949 or thereabouts. Any mistakes on the part of the leaders might have caused a postponement of victory. Forty or fifty years is but a fleeting moment in the long process of history. Although there were many colonial countries in the East with historical conditions similar to those in

China, after decades of struggle only China won a complete victory. In some countries, the people's forces became very powerful for a time, but they were almost wiped out overnight owing to mistakes on the part of their leaders.

Speaking about the strategy of war, Chairman Mao said, "The stage of action for a military man is built upon objective material conditions, but on that stage he can direct the performance of many a drama, full of sound and color, power and grandeur." Where conditions permit, a competent commander can direct the performance of many a drama, full of power and grandeur. If the commander is not competent, the performance may turn out to be a failure. The Chinese revolution was a drama with the loudest sound, the richest color, and the greatest power and grandeur, because, on the one hand, conditions permitted this, and on the other, the subjective force of the revolution played a great role. The subjective force here refers mainly to the role of the leaders, and among the leaders Chairman Mao's role was the greatest.

Secondly, I said in my article that during the rectification movement Chairman Mao criticized those inside the Party "who cannot open their mouths without citing ancient Greece," and that "ancient Greece" here might refer to the Soviet Union. Some comrades asked if I had made this assertion on good grounds. I must admit that I inferred this and it would be difficult to obtain clear and unambiguous proof. However, I believe my inference is not without foundation. People who are skeptical about my inference are of the opinion that "ancient Greece" in this context might refer to foreign countries in general, implying that some people knew a great deal about foreign countries but little about China. In the 1930s there were already those who advocated total Westernization. If Chairman Mao had in mind foreign countries in general, he might have said they "cannot open their mouths without citing Britain and America." In this way people would have known that Chairman Mao was directing his criticism at total Westernization, i. e., bourgeois liberalization. However, in this case Chairman Mao was not criticizing total Westernization, but people within the Party and among the ranks of Marxists, who could not be referred to by the statement "people who cannot open their mouths without citing Britain and America." Given the circumstances at the time, it was not appropriate to pinpoint the Soviet Union by name. The statement "who cannot open their mouths without citing ancient Greece" was thus a really clever rhetorical device.

Thirdly, in my article I quoted Chairman Mao as saying that Stalin did a number of wrong things in connection with China, "In 1949 and 1950 the pressure on us was very strong indeed." Some comrades asked me what the pressure was and in what ways this pressure was manifested.

This question is worth discussing and we should link it to the remark "Stalin did a number of wrong things in connection with China." It could be said that the attitude of the Soviet Union was very ambiguous when the Chinese revolution achieved victory. Here I will only cite one example. According to the reminiscences of the American correspondent Anna Louise Strong, in October 1948 when she arrived in Moscow via Western Europe, the victory of the Chinese Communist Party was making front-page headlines in the international press although nothing at all appeared in Soviet newspapers. It was not until the beginning of November that four or five lines appeared under " Tass Announcements" on the last page of *Pravda* announcing the capture of Shenyang by the Chinese People's Liberation Army (PLA). This was the Liaoxi-Shenyang Campaign that lasted from 12 September to 2 November 1948. On 6 December, under "Tass Announcements" on the fourth page there was a short news item announcing that the PLA had captured Xuzhou. This was the Huaihai Campaign from 6 November 1948 to 10 January 1949. [1] The Soviet Union, just as Chairman Mao said, adopted a skeptical attitude towards China when we won the war.

Comrade Liu Shaoqi paid a secret visit to the Soviet Union in the late summer-early autumn of 1949. On 16 December the same year, Chairman Mao went to Moscow, a visit that was publicly announced. At that time the Chinese had just achieved victory, the founding of the People's Republic of China had been proclaimed to the world, and Mao Zedong was the top leader of the Party and state in China, his visit should therefore have been an official state visit. However, Chairman Mao actually went to Moscow to congratulate Stalin on his birthday. He stayed for two full months, from 16 December 1949 to 17 February 1950. It is true that transport facilities were not as good as today, but this two-month stay was a little too long. The reception ceremony was relatively formal, but Stalin addressed Chairman Mao as "Mr. Mao Zedong". Apart from his participa-

---

[ 1 ] See *Reminiscences of Anna Louise Strong on Why the Russian Arrested Me And Its Possible Relation to China.*

tion in the celebrations for Stalin's birthday, Mao Zedong was left out in the cold, no one paid any attention to him, and there was no report of his visit in the Soviet press. The Western press circulated a rumor that Stalin had placed Mao Zedong under house arrest. Mao waited in Moscow until 2 January when Vyacheslav Molotov came for a discussion. What was the matter? As it turned out, Stalin did not want to sign a treaty of alliance, mutual assistance and cooperation with New China. Was there not already a treaty with China? he asked, referring to the treaty signed with the Kuomintang. Since a treaty already existed there was no need for a new one. Stalin's idea was to "put the matter aside for now". When Chairman Mao and Molotov met, Mao presented several alternatives, the last of which was to sign a new treaty. Molotov asked for instructions from Stalin, who agreed to sign a new treaty. Chairman Mao then said that he would ask Zhou Enlai to come to Moscow for discussion of the treaty.

Chairman Mao was very angry about the Soviet attitude. On one occasion he flew into a rage and said that he had come to Moscow for only three reasons: to eat, to shit and to sleep. Many foreigners knew about this. We can also see from the telegrams sent by Chairman Mao from Moscow at that time, and the many directed to him, that he was actually handling domestic affairs while in Moscow. Problems also cropped up during discussions on the treaty. The Soviet side presented a draft treaty to Premier Zhou, which was basically the treaty signed by the Soviet Union with the Kuomintang. After consultation with Chairman Mao, Premier Zhou put forward a new draft as the basis for discussion.

In addition to the treaty, the Soviet government

provided China with a loan to the tune of US $ 300 million. The Western press reported that the loan was less than that given by the Soviet Union to Poland not long before. I do not know who decided on the amount of the loan, but Chairman Mao sent a telegram at that time from Moscow to the Central Committee of the Chinese Communist Party, saying we should borrow less. We can thus see that Chairman Mao was very unhappy about his visit to Moscow. If we relate this visit to other events that occurred both before and after it, we can see that it was not strange for Chairman Mao to feel that the pressure was very great in 1949 and 1950.

Fourthly, I said in my article that Chairman Mao always took a skeptical attitude towards or firmly opposed an economic structure in which there was an overconcentration of power and everything was managed under state plans. Some comrades asked me if I said this on good grounds, and whether I had deliberately advertised the fact that during his life Chairman Mao was opposed to a planned economy, now that China is ushering in a socialist market economy.

It is true that in the past we adopted the Soviet model of a planned economy. Comrade Deng Xiaoping said, "We used to copy foreign models [" *foreign models*" *here of course refers to the Soviet model* ] mechanically, which only hampered the development of our productive forces, induced ideological rigidity and kept the people and grass-roots units from taking any initiative." This was a comment on the past. However, he added at once that "We made some mistakes of our own as well, such as the 'Great Leap Forwardand' and the 'cultural revolution,' which were our own inventions." We therefore had two types of mistakes: the mistake of copying foreign models and mistakes of our own invention. It was mainly Chairman Mao who advocated not copying foreign models, and it was Chairman Mao who tried to use the Great Leap Forward to break down the planned economy, but his method did not work and he failed. For example, in 1958 China introduced a method of setting two targets for the state plan, the first target was obligatory and the second aspired to. The central government had two targets, so did the provincial governments. The second target of the central government became the first target of the provincial governments. In the eyes of the Soviets who saw planning as law, this practice was downright nonsense. The "Great Leap Forward" did not succeed. So we copied foreign models anyway in our practical economic tasks.

However, Chairman Mao was always dissatisfied with the planned economy, and unhappy with this way of doing things. He once quoted Li Qingzhao (李清照), a female poet of the Song dynasty, in describing the planned economy: "Looking hither and thither/ Cold and dreary/ Oh, it's so sorrowful and melancholy! " In his *A Review of Some Important Policy Decisions and Events*, Comrade Bo Yibo (薄一波) said that Chairman Mao emphatically pointed out that, "It is a revolution to change the way of planned economy. Once you copied the Soviet model and got used to it, it seems very difficult to change. " Chairman Mao was indeed dissatisfied with the planned economy, but he failed to find a correct way of replacing the Soviet model.

Fifthly, some comrades have pointed out that it was wrong for me to say that so many detours and mistakes were made as a result of the independent search for our own road and that it is now meaningless to discuss whether or not these detours and mistakes could have been avoided. What I really wanted to say is that it is useless to feel dejected by these detours and mistakes or, to put it another way, it is no good crying over spilt milk, however, I failed to say this clearly. Of course it is significant to study the causes of past mistakes in order to avoid further mistakes in the future. However, I immediately stated that it is meaningless to suppose that it would have been better for us to take the road we are now following directly from 1957 instead of as late as 1978. I am still of the opinion that it was impossible in 1957 for China to find the road it has been following since 1978. The extent and duration of these detours and mistakes were determined by a variety of factors and we cannot say they were inevitable.

Sixthly, some comrades have also asked the following question: If we say the "Leftist" mistakes made for 20 years after 1957 were the result of exploration, can we also say that the "Leftist" mistakes made before the Zunyi Meeting in the democratic revolution were the result of exploration? Did Wang Ming make his mistakes in the course of his exploration? It is true that Wang Ming's mistakes in the 1930s constituted an important lesson for the Communist Party of China and that the Party formulated its correct line on the basis of the lesson drawn from Wang Ming's mistakes after the Zunyi Meeting, but these mistakes were not made during the course of exploration. On the contrary, Wang did not proceed from the national conditions in China, but copied the Soviet model and blindly followed directions from the Soviet Union and the Communist International. Wang Ming's mistakes and those made by the Party after 1957 were therefore totally different. The mistakes after 1957 were made at a time when China was looking for its own road, not copying foreign models and not bowing to the foreign baton, but we fell onto the wrong path.

Seventhly, in the last part of my article I mentioned that a few months before he passed away Chairman Mao said that he had done two things in his life. He said this on 13 June and I do not know how I confused the date and it became 30 April. This should be corrected. The year before last when I wrote *Seventy Years of the Communist Party of China* Comrade Hu Qiaomu (胡乔木) asked me to cite these words in my book to prove that Chairman Mao had lost confidence in the "cultural revolution" during his last days. However, if I had included these words I would have had to say more, and because space was limited, I did not cite this remark. Following Comrade Hu Qiaomu's suggestion, I included these words in my article although I did not cite the passage in full. Chairman Mao said that the second thing he had done was the "cultural revolution", to which few people gave their support and many raised objections. These lines might not be enough to prove that he had lost confidence in the "cultural revolution". However, in the few sentences that follow these lines Mao Zedong said, "Neither of the two things has been finished. I will hand over this legacy to the next generation. It seems there will not be a peaceful hand-over. The hand-over might be carried out in disturbance; and if things go wrong, there will be a bloodbath on the battlefield." These lines reveal that three months before his death Chairman Mao was in very poor health and feeling very sad. The laws of nature made it impossible for him to live longer and have more energy, otherwise he would have reconsidered these problems.

Eighthly, I would like to mention briefly the struggle against Soviet great-nation chauvinism in the 1960s. There were, in fact, thorny problems in two areas between China and the Soviet Union. One area involved ideological problems, including their different views on the international situation, the international communist movement and their external and internal policies. The other problem was the Soviet attempt to control China, or the problem of the patriarchal party as we called it then. The Soviet Union regarded itself as the foremost authority in the world and waved its baton at other countries, forcing them to obey its strategy of cooperation with the United States to dominate the world, and thus bringing them into the orbit of its global strategy. These different views constituted an ideological problem, and it was the practice of a patriarchal party to demand obedience from other parties.

Given the circumstances at that time, I would like to say that Chairman Mao was very careful with regard to the ideological problems. In 1956, many in China were dissatisfied with the Communist Party of the Soviet Union because of its total rejection of Stalin at its Twentieth Congress; yet Chairman Mao said the Twentieth Congress exposed Stalin's hidden problems and this point should be affirmed. In the following year, Khrushchev labeled Molotov and others as an anti-party clique and removed them from office. This caused discontent among some comrades of the older generation in our Party, but Chairman Mao said that this was their own party's affair and that Molotov and his ilk were rigid-minded and might not be much better than Khrushchev. Many comrades thought that Khrushchev was a revisionist, while Chairman Mao said that we should wait and see, perhaps he was only semi-revisionist. It can thus be seen that Chairman Mao was very careful about these problems.

However, in relation to problems involving China's independence and sovereignty, Chairman Mao made no concessions. In 1958 the Soviet side proposed the joint establishment with China of long-wave radio stations and a joint fleet. In fact, the Soviet Union tried to take military, and then political, control of our country. Chairman Mao firmly resisted and made no compromise. When China later tried to maintain normal state relations with the Soviet Union, Chairman Mao said that quarrels did not matter, even if they continued for a thousand years, meaning that in spite of ideological differences and quarrels, the two countries could maintain normal relations as long as the Communist Party of the Soviet Union did not pose as a patriarchal party and handled relations between the two sides on the basis of e-quality. (It seems now that it would have been better not to quarrel over ideological problems.) Liu Shaoqi and Deng Xiaoping went to Moscow at that time and also quarreled with the Soviet side, mainly over the problem of the patriarchal party. The Soviet Communist Party could not openly claim to be a patriarchal party and therefore always tried to highlight ideological differences in an attempt to cover its true features. China later placed more emphasis on ideology; in my view Chen Bo-da(陈伯达) and Kang Sheng(康生) played a greater part in this regard.

Commenting on this episode in 1980, Comrade Deng Xiaoping said, "If a Party and the country which it leads pursue a foreign policy of interference in the internal affairs of other countries, or invasion or subversion of them, then any other Party is entitled to make its stand known and express its criticism. We have always opposed the Communist party of the Soviet Union acting like a patriarchal party and displaying great-power chauvinism. It pursues a hegemonist line and policy in foreign relations. "[1] At that time, the Soviet Union asked all socialist states to follow its lead in their domestic policies and tried to take political and economic control of them in the name of a "socialist community". It demanded obedience to its diplomatic strategy from other countries, and even went so far as to interfere with the selection of the leaders in other countries. It could not be said that the communist parties of Eastern Europe had done nothing for the people of their own countries, one of the main reasons that they lost the support of the people was that, in the eyes of the people, they had reduced their countries to dependencies and satellite states.

From the late 1950s, Chairman Mao firmly resisted the pressure of Soviet great-nation chauvinism, and tried to break with the Soviet model and search for China's own road to socialist construction. He failed to find a correct road for China and fell onto the wrong path, but he will go down in history as a great pioneer in this exploration. His first achievement which is related to the second will in any case become more illustrious with time.

---

[1] Deng Xiaoping, *ibid.*, pp. 300-301.

# What Is Socialism and How Is It to Be Constructed?

## —Notes on Volume Three of the *Selected Works of Deng Xiaoping*

Deng Xiaoping said, "The realization of socialism and communism was the lofty ideal we Marxists set for ourselves during the revolutionary years. Now that we are trying to reform the economy, we shall continue to keep to the socialist road and to uphold the ideal of communism. This is something our younger generation in particular must understand. But the problem is: What is socialism and how is it to be built? The most important lesson we have learned, among a great many others, is that we must be clear about those questions. "[1]What new important ideas have been put forward by Comrade Deng Xiaoping with regard to these questions? This article will make a tentative analysis in this regard.

The works of Deng Xiaoping are not textbooks and therefore do not set out general definitions and make general explanations. Deng Xiaoping has been seeking, not universally applicable formulas, but the solutions to practical problems, practical problems encountered during socialist construction in China. He said, "By Marx-

---

[1] Deng Xiaoping, *Selected Works*, Beijing, Foreign Languages Press, 1994, Vol. III, p. 122

ism we mean Marxism that is integrated with Chinese conditions, and by socialism we mean a socialism that is tailored to Chinese conditions and has a specifically Chinese character. "[1]

However, we must also find out the new content with which Deng Xiaoping's works have enriched the Marxist theory of scientific socialism. With a view to solving practical problems, he has summed up the historical experience of socialism in China, and also in the world, and put forward a series of new Marxist viewpoints. The Marxist theory of socialism is an evergreen tree, which develops and is enriched with practice; Deng Xiaoping has made great contributions in this regard.

In this paper I will discuss four associated questions:

1. The development of productive forces;
2. The primary stage of socialism;
3. The reform—emancipation of productive forces;
4. A socialist market economy.

## I. The Development of Productive Forces

Deng Xiaoping said in 1986, "The principles of socialism are: first, development of production, and second, common prosperity. "[2] He elaborated on this view during his inspection tour of south China in the spring of 1992, "The essence of socialism is liberation and development of the productive forces, elimination of poverty and polarization, and the ultimate achievement

---

[1] *Ibid.*, p. 73.
[2] *Ibid.*, p. 174.

of prosperity for all. "[1]

Deng Xiaoping has always emphasized that development of productive forces must be placed before everything else, and has stressed this point over and again. He said, "The fundamental task for the socialist stage is to develop the productive forces. "[2]"The primary task in the socialist period is to develop the productive forces and gradually improve people's material and cultural life. "[3] His remarks concerning the emancipation of productive forces through reform under socialist conditions is related to the demand for the development of productive forces.

In refutation of the fallacy proposed by the "Gang of Four"(四人帮) during the "cultural revolution" that "it is better to be poor under socialism than to be rich under capitalism", Deng Xiaoping stated categorically that poverty is not socialism. In addition to refuting this absurdity of the "Gang of Four," this statement was also aimed at a shortcoming that had long existed in the Party's guiding principles. Deng said, "One of our shortcomings after the founding of the People's Republic was that we didn't pay enough attention to developing the productive forces. "[4] Therefore, he added, "Our experience in the 20 years from 1958 to 1978 teaches us that poverty is not socialism, that socialism means eliminating poverty. Unless you are developing the productive forces and raising people's living standards, you cannot say that you are building socialism. "[5]

---

[1] *Ibid.*, p. 361.
[2] *Ibid.*, p. 73.
[3] *Ibid.*, p. 122.
[4] *Ibid.*, p. 122.
[5] *Ibid.*, p. 73.

The idea that "the trouble does not lie in poverty but in inequality" had a far-reaching effect in Chinese history. Peasant uprisings in feudal society, based on the original low level of productive forces, inevitably had egalitarianism as their goal. This egalitarianism was, so to speak, also a kind of poor socialism; it played a positive role in history, but is completely detrimental in modern times.

Placing the development of productive forces before everything else does not mean that socialism aims only to develop productive forces. Deng Xiaoping said, "One of the features distinguishing socialism from capitalism is that socialism means common prosperity, not polarization of income. The wealth created belongs first to the state and second to the people; it is therefore impossible for a new bourgeoisie to emerge."[1]

Public ownership is indispensable to socialism, so is the system of distribution to each according to his work. He said, "... predominance of public ownership and common prosperity are the two fundamental socialist principles that we must adhere to."[2] He also said, "In China a bourgeoisie will not emerge during the process of development, because our principle of distribution is to each according to his work."[3]

Some people ask whether the objective of socialism is public ownership or the development of productive forces? One answer to the question is that only when public ownership is taken as the objective can the socialist road be firmly adhered to; the other answer is that,

---

[1] *Ibid.*, p. 129.
[2] *Ibid.*, p. 117.
[3] *Ibid.*, p. 250.

in order to show the importance we place on developing productive forces, we should take this as the objective and public ownership as the means. In my view, the question is not posited in the correct way, and neither answer is completely correct. If the objective referred to here means the ultimate aim of socialism, then it is neither public ownership nor the development of productive forces, but the general improvement of the material and cultural life of people throughout the society (until, finally, communism is realized), that is, in Deng Xiaoping's words, common prosperity. Deng has often spoken of this goal of common prosperity. For example, he said, "The aim of socialism is to make all our people prosperous, not to create polarization."[1] To ensure the realization of common prosperity, there must be both development of productive forces and public ownership, since if public ownership is abandoned, development of productive forces would result in the prosperity of only a few and polarization of income; on the other hand, without development of productive forces, public ownership would mean common poverty.

Before the birth of Marxism, Utopian socialism of every hue advocated public ownership. It should be said that the socialist ideal is associated with this demand for public ownership; without public ownership there will be no socialism. But socialist thinkers of the past all envisaged public ownership on the basis of a low level of productive forces and advocated, with few exceptions, poor socialism. One of the characteristics of Marxist scientific socialism is that it strives to put public ownership on the basis of highly developed productive forces, more

[1] *Ibid.*,p. 116.

developed than under capitalism. Marx and Engels said in *Manifesto of the Communist Party* that the proletariat would increase the total productive forces as rapidly as possible after it took over political rule. Deng Xiaoping also said, "Marxism attaches utmost importance to developing the productive forces. "[1] Therefore, eliminating the worship of poor public ownership and poor socialism conforms with Marxist principles.

On the question of the development of productive forces, Deng Xiaoping does not just repeat the words of the founders of Marxism, but enriches Marxism with new ideas. He proposed making the development of productive forces the central task, and suggested that the development of public ownership and the system of distribution to each according to his work be subordinated to the development of productive forces.

Deng Xiaoping said, "Comrade Mao Zedong was a great leader, and it was under his leadership that the Chinese revolution triumphed. Unfortunately, however, he made the grave mistake of neglecting the development of the productive forces. I do not mean that he didn't want to develop them. The point is, not all the methods he used were correct. For instance, neither the initiation of the 'Great Leap Forward' nor the people's commune conformed to the laws governing socio-economic development. "[2] Deng Xiaoping here reveals the reasons why Mao Zedong and the party neglected the development of productive forces. Numerous remarks could be cited to show that Mao Zedong and other leading comrades wanted very much to develop productive

---

[1] *Ibid.*,p. 73.
[2] *Ibid.*,p. 122.

forces, but they used incorrect methods and, as a result, overlooked or neglected the development of productive forces.

Only when we do things according to the laws of economic development can we really promote the development of productive forces. This idea involves the following two aspects:

Firstly, the development of productive forces has its own laws. The political enthusiasm of the masses inspired by the birth of socialism may play an important role in the development of society, but it cannot be transformed into modern productive forces without the agency of science and technology. Deng Xiaoping pointed out as far back as 1975 that science and technology are part of the productive forces, and later he said that they should be seen as a primary productive force. To make people exert greater efforts in their work is certainly one of the roles politics plays in the development of productive forces, but the primary role should be to stimulate people to acquire knowledge of science and technology. Mao Zedong started the "Great Leap Forward" in 1958, thinking China would go forward by leaps and bounds if only the enthusiasm of the masses was aroused and the people were made to exert greater effort in their work. In the end things turned out contrary to his wishes. In cases like this politics rather than the development of productive forces took precedence, with the result that the aim of developing productive forces was thwarted and the role of politics was distorted.

Another aspect is the relationship between the development of productive forces and the development of the relations of production. Deng Xiaoping stressed the predominance of productive forces. This ran counter to the mistaken view prevalent both in China and abroad over the previous decades that, since the relations of production in a system of socialist public ownership are advanced, once formed they should be maintained intact and productive forces will develop steadily; if the productive forces do not develop rapidly enough, attempts must be made to make the relations of production more "advanced". Historical experience has shown that this view is impractical and not conducive to the development of socialism.

Stalin believed that relations of production and productive forces were completely compatible under socialism and therefore the problem of improving the relations of production would never arise. Mao Zedong did not agree with Stalin's ossified thinking, but he did not solve the problem the right way. In the course of his search for a better solution, at least when he decided to set up the rural people's communes, he tried to develop productive forces with a more progressive form of socialist relations of production, and stressed that the progressiveness of the commune was that it was "large and public". However, experience demonstrated that the people's communes could not bring about an advance in productive forces although they seemed progressive in form.

After the initial establishment of socialist relations of production, priority should be given to the development of productive forces. The socialist system of public ownership and the related system of distribution in which each is paid according to the work done are, generally speaking, advanced, but the extent to which this system is applied and the specific forms the system takes must depend on the development of productive forces. That is to say, the specific forms of the socialist relations of production must change with the development of productive forces and must conform to the requirements of this development. Whether a specific form is right or not depends on whether it promotes the development of productive forces, rather than whether it is larger and more public.

Summing up historical experience, Deng Xiaoping courageously advanced the idea of giving first priority to the development of productive forces. This is a creative Marxist view. He highlighted this view when reform of the rural structure had only just begun. By 1980, several provinces had already changed the people's commune system into the household contract responsibility system with remuneration linked to output and achieved good results. But many provinces had still not carried out this reform or were only just beginning to do so. In a talk on questions of rural policy at the end of May 1980, Deng Xiaoping said, "Some comrades are worried that this practice may have an adverse effect on the collective economy. I think their fears are unwarranted. Development of the collective economy continues to be our general objective. . . . It is certain that as long as production expands, division of labor increases and the commodity economy develops, lower forms of collectivization in the countryside will develop into higher forms and the collective economy will acquire a firmer basis. The key task is to expand the productive forces and thereby create conditions for the further development of collectivization. "[1] That is to say, the development of productive

---

[ 1 ] Deng Xiaoping, *Selected Works* (1975—1982), p. 297.

forces will promote the development of the relations of production under socialism. If we pursue the "progressive" system of public ownership in accordance with abstract criteria and ignore the development of productive forces, believing this will promote the development of productive forces, we will surely be led astray.

It is of great significance given China's historical conditions to establish the principles that priority should be given to the development of productive forces, that the relations of production must be compatible with the development of productive forces, and that the superiority of socialism should find expression in the development of productive forces. These principles are applicable not only to China but may be of universal significance. However, Deng Xiaoping does not put forward these principles in a general way, but applies them to the realities of China. He not only asked the whole party and the whole country to unswervingly take the development of productive forces as their central task, but also, on the basis that China is still in the primary stage of socialism, posed a series of important questions related to the development of productive forces and the socialist system.

## II. The Primary Stage of Socialism

The Communist Party of China stressed at its Thirteenth Congress convened in October 1987 that the party should adopt the proposition that China is in the primary stage of socialism as the starting point for all its work. Deng Xiaoping said to a foreign visitor two months before that, "The Thirteenth National Party Congress will explain what stage China is in: the primary stage of socialism. Socialism itself is the first stage of communism, and here in China we are still in the primary stage of socialism — that is, the underdeveloped stage. In everything we do we must proceed from this reality, and all planning must be consistent with it. "[1]

For many years socialism has been generally perceived as a rather short transitional period before communism, and therefore it seems unnecessary to divide socialism into stages. Historical experience has shown this view to be wrong.

According to the vision of Marx and Engels, revolution would take place in the advanced capitalist countries and give birth to socialism. Whether socialism would have a primary and an advanced stage even in these countries is a question open to discussion. In countries like China with a very backward economy, socialism will inevitably be a long historical period, beginning with the primary stage. Therefore, the Chinese Communist Party put forward the scientific concept of the primary stage of socialism, not in a general sense but based on the national conditions of China.

Mao Zedong and the generation of leaders represented by him were at times impatient to leap into communism and made the mistake of trying to plunge ahead too fast. Although they believed socialism would endure for a long period in China, and Mao Zedong even divided socialism into two stages, underdeveloped and developed, they did not proceed from the reality of China being in the primary stage of socialism when they tackled China's problems. Deng Xiaoping said, "China suffered greatly from the ten-year disaster, the 'cultural revolu-

---

[ 1 ]   Deng Xiaoping, *Selected Works*, Vol. III, p. 248.

tion. ' In fact, not just from that, as early as the second half of 1957 we began to make 'Left' mistakes. To put it briefly, we pursued a closed-door policy in foreign affairs and took class struggle as the central ask at home. No attempt was made to expand productive forces, and the policies we formulated were too ambitious for the primary stage of socialism. "[1] All the general and specific policies formulated after the Third Plenary Session of the Eleventh Central Committee of the Chinese Communist Party are based on the lessons drawn from the past mistake of attempting to transcend the primary stage of socialism.

Deng Xiaoping believes that in order to carry out the four modernizations in China we must take into account at least two important features of our situation: one is that we are starting from a weak base, the other is that we have a large population but not enough arable land. He said in 1979 in connection with the first feature that, since the founding of the People's Republic, we had achieved signal successes in economic construction, nevertheless, because of our low starting point, China was still one of the world's poor countries; generally speaking, we are 20 to 30 years behind the advanced countries in the overall development of science and technology. Mao Zedong and the other leaders of his times also understood that China was building socialism on the basis of poverty and backwardness. Mao Zedong generalized this situation with the words "poor and blank". However, they underestimated the difficulties and even argued that on the basis of being "poor and blank" the freshest and most beautiful pictures could be painted.

---

[1] *Ibid.*, p. 264.

Referring to the "Great Leap Forward" in 1958, Comrade Bo Yibo said in *A Review of Some Important Policy Decisions and Events* that people generally believed "China, though so economically and culturally backward and so big, would have fulfilled the task of socialist construction and started the transition from socialism to communism after three years' hard struggle and several years' construction." He also said, "The lopsided view of taking poverty and blankness as an advantage also had a role in playing down the arduousness of the task to change the backwardness of China."[1]

Practice demonstrated that Mao Zedong's argument was unrealistic. The freshest and most beautiful pictures of socialism must necessarily be associated with highly developed productive forces, and there will be no fresh and beautiful pictures to speak of if productive forces are underdeveloped. The significance of the theory of the primary stage of socialism is that it clearly indicates that we must formulate our principles and policies in accordance with the realities of the primary stage of socialism, and should not rigidly adhere to socialism in its general form. In other words, we should not take socialism in its abstract and pure form as the basis for judgment.

In the period of democratic revolution, Mao Zedong proceeded from the specific conditions in China and found a correct road for the Chinese revolution. In the eyes of those who rigidly stuck to the general formulas of Marxism, this road was absurd. Indeed if we had not taken specific conditions into consideration, and simply

---

[1] Bo Yibo, *A Review of Some Important Policy Decisions and Events*, Chinese edition, p. 720.

asked whether the cities or the countryside should be taken as the base for a democratic revolution led by the proletariat, the question would have been difficult to answer. However, under the specific historical conditions in China, the only correct way was for the political party of the proletariat to go to the countryside, mobilize the broad masses of the peasants for armed struggle and encircle the cities from the countryside.

The case is similar with socialist construction. Now that we are building socialism on the foundation of being "poor and blank", we must admit that China is currently in the primary stage of socialism, which in turn demands that we must pay more attention to the development of productive forces, and, to this end, adopt principles and policies that are in tune with the primary stage of socialism. Deng Xiaoping said, "We should not be restricted by conventional thinking. Our heads used to be full of conventional ideas, but now we have broken free of them."[1] "Conventional thinking" here includes the general socialist formulas found in books, and "breaking free of them" means we should integrate Marx's general principles related to socialism with the specific conditions in China during the primary stage of socialism, and break free of the general formulas. Like Mao Zedong, who dared to break free of conventional thinking and found the road to victory in the Chinese democratic revolution, Deng Xiaoping has dared to break free of conventional thinking and found the road to building socialism with Chinese characteristics, both of them displaying great theoretical courage.

Many problems would have remained unsolved if we

---

[1]  Deng Xiaoping, *Selected Works*, Vol. III, p. 255.

had been restricted by conventional thinking. From 1978, the system of people's communes was changed into the household contract responsibility system with remuneration linked to output. "When we proposed instituting the household contract responsibility system with the remuneration linked to output, many people disagreed and doubted that the system was socialist."[1] If specific historical conditions are not taken into consideration, and we ask which of the two forms of ownership —the people's communes in which all the means of production were publicly-owned, or the household contract system—is more socialist, it is difficult to answer. Historical experience has shown that, although the ownership system of the people's commune (which later reverted to a three-tiered system of ownership—the commune, the production brigade and the production team—with the production teams owning the most) seemed more socialist, it failed to develop productive forces in rural areas or to raise the living standards of the peasants. On the other hand, the household contract responsibility system with remuneration linked to output (combined with a double operational structure) has opened up broader prospects for development in the socialist countryside in China.

As early as 1978 Deng Xiaoping advocated that "... We should allow some regions and enterprises and some workers and peasants to earn more and enjoy more benefits sooner than others, in accordance with their hard work and greater contributions to society." He believed that "those are major policies which can have an effect

---

[1] *Ibid.*, p. 354.

on the whole national economy and push it forward. "[1]
He has repeatedly talked about this proposition after-
wards. For example, he said in February 1984, "We
shall allow some areas to become rich first; egalitarianism will not work. This is a cardinal policy, and I hope
all of you will give it some thought. "[2] We have
worked in this way over the past decade and achieved
good results. Viewed in the abstract, it seems strange
to have put forward such major policies. As socialism
advocates common prosperity, it might seem inappropriate to let some regions and people get rich first. However, if seen from the perspective of the practical conditions of socialism in its primary stage, such policies are
understandable and necessary. China is a very big country and great differences exist between various regions;
if they were to move in step, they would all fall into the
quagmire of poverty resulting from the search for equality.

Another very important policy is maintaining the
predominance of public ownership but at the same time
allowing the existence of various non-public economies.
Deng Xiaoping said, "We allow the development of individual economies, of joint ventures with both Chinese
and foreign investment and enterprises wholly owned by
foreign businessmen, but socialist public ownership will
always remain predominant. "[3] With regard to foreign
funds, he said, "Our socialist economic base is so huge
that it can absorb tens of hundreds of billions of dollars'
worth of foreign funds without being shaken. Foreign

---

[1] Deng Xiaoping, *Selected Works* (1975—1982), pp. 163—164.
[2] Deng Xiaoping, *Selected Works*, Vol. III, p. 62.
[3] *Ibid.*, p. 116.

investment will doubtless serve as a major supplement in the building of socialism in our country. And as things stand now, that supplement is indispensable. "[1] In light of this and according to specific historical conditions in Hong Kong, Macao and Taiwan, he put forward the unprecedented proposition of "one country, two system". He said, "The main part of China must continue under socialism, but a capitalist system will be allowed to exist in certain areas, such as Hong Kong and Taiwan. "[2] "The fact that one billion people, the overwhelming majority in a vast area, live under socialism is the indispensable precondition that enables us to allow capitalism in these small, limited areas at our side. We believe the existence of capitalism in limited areas will actually be conducive to the development of socialism. "[3]

It seems only common sense not to "go by the book" in building socialism. But it is very difficult to put this principle into effect. Deng Xiaoping's ideas, as mentioned above, just like Mao Zedong's idea of encircling the cities from the countryside in his time, are bound to be viewed by dogmatists as absurd, and as a departure from the right track. Deng Xiaoping emphasized that Marxism should not be taken as a dogma and must be developed. He said, "Our revolution triumphed because we encircled the cities from the rural areas, although that strategy is not to be found in Marxist-Leninist books. Today we still uphold Marxism-Leninism and Mao Zedong Thought, part of which we have

---

[1] *Ibid.*, p. 74—75.
[2] *Ibid.*, p. 69.
[3] *Ibid.*, p. 109.

inherited and part of which we have developed ourselves. We are building socialism, or to be more precise, we are building a socialism suited to conditions in China. In this way we are truly adhering to Marxism. "[1]

In their writings, Marx and Engels postulated a socialist system of the future. Since they drew on rational elements of the socialist aspirations of generations of advanced people, and, in particular, studied the history of the birth and development of capitalism and revealed the inevitability of its demise, their postulation is scientific. However, they could only draw a rough outline of the socialist system. Although Lenin took initial steps towards socialism, he was not in a position to advance systematic ideas on its construction. Deng Xiaoping said, "The socialist system is one thing, and the specific way of building socialism another. " [2] If we substitute the concept of highly developed socialism, even though it is quite correct, for the long process of exploration during the construction of socialism, we will surely accomplish nothing. We must march along the socialist road in our drive for modernization, but we should not rigidly adhere to basic socialist concepts and always take them as the guide for our actions. We have to proceed from the actual conditions of our country and take various measures conducive to the development of productive forces; otherwise our socialist cause will not prosper.

In the past we differentiated between capitalism and socialism according to abstract concepts and suffered a great deal as a result. We believed for a time that since

---

[ 1 ] *Ibid.*, p. 191.
[ 2 ] Deng Xiaoping, *Selected Works* (1975—1982), p. 235.

we were building socialism everything generated in capitalist society should be rejected. Moreover, we held that socialism meant doing everything according to the ideal socialist model and rejecting anything that was not compatible with socialist criteria. The once prevalent slogan "Foster proletarian ideology and eliminate bourgeois ideology" was brandished in this spirit. Deng Xiaoping said, "As I see it now, however, this old slogan is neither comprehensive nor precise enough. For lack of sufficient investigation and analysis, certain comrades have criticized as 'capitalism' some of our current reforms, which are useful to the development of production and the socialist cause as a whole. They are wrong in this."[1]

### III. Reform — Emancipation of Productive Forces

Like any social morphology during the history of mankind, it was impossible for socialism to be born mature and perfect, and to grow and develop without undergoing any change in its economic, political and social systems.

There has never been a society in any country that was immutable from beginning to end, be it a slave society, a feudal society or a capitalist society. The ruling class of a society in which class exploitation exists, when seeing social evils and the need for change in the economic, political and social systems, will take resolute action to bring about these changes, this is called reform. What differentiates reform from revolution in a society in which there is class exploitation is that revolu-

---

[1]  *Ibid.*, p. 321.

tion is carried out by the ruled class while reform is carried out by the ruling class; if a revolution succeeds, the society will change from one morphology to another, but reform is a change in the same social morphology. (There have been instances in human history in which reform led to a change of social morphology, e. g., from a slave society to a feudal society, and from a feudal society into a capitalist society. This is because the two different social morphologies belong to the same category of society, i. e., a society of class exploitation). The "New Deal" carried out from 1929 onwards by American President Franklin D. Roosevelt during the economic crisis was one of the major reforms in the history of capitalist development. It drew attention from all over the world as soon as it was proposed. At that time, some people even suspected that Roosevelt was going to transform capitalism into socialism, but in fact he only implemented reform within the framework of the capitalist system. This reform enabled capitalism to ride through the crisis and brought its remaining vitality into full play. Many reforms of varying depth have taken place in the capitalist world in the past 300 or 400 years since the birth of capitalism. The history of this period is worth reviewing.

The establishment of socialist society indicates that the people are creating a new society with an unprecedented consciousness based on their understanding of the general laws of social development. However, no one can foretell the details of such development. Therefore, people cannot build socialism in the way that builders construct a new house according to a perfect blueprint. Like other societies, socialist society inevitably changes during the long period of its existence along with the development of productive forces and other objective realities. Furthermore, possible mistakes in understanding on the part of those constructing socialism will make the developmental process of the new society even more tortuous. Historical experience has shown that when objective conditions change and the builder's mistakes need to be corrected, the construction of socialism will ultimately fail if reform is not introduced in time.

It can be seen from the above that the need for reform commonly arises during the process of the development of socialist society. The reforms carried out in China are based on the experience of socialism in China over more than twenty years, beginning in the late 1950s, as well as those of international socialist construction, led by the former Soviet Union for more than sixty years, from the late 1920s onwards. In this historical period, much positive experience was gained from the socialist construction in various countries, but at the same time weaknesses were exposed that were difficult to avoid in the process of building socialism in those countries without a background of developed capitalism; man's distorted understanding of socialism under such historical conditions was also revealed. A serious warning was issued to the effect that socialism would be doomed if reforms were not introduced or not carried out in the right way.

To put it briefly, the drawbacks in the economic and political structures of the countries concerned with socialist construction during this historical period were as follows:

1. All of these countries relied too much on centralized state power, which was used to manage and control every aspect of national life, with the result that the

state had to bear too heavy a burden and the initiative of all sectors except the state was not brought into full play or was even stifled.

2. They did not draw on the achievements of capitalism that could be used, either directly or with modifications, to serve socialism.

This socialist model reflected man's incorrect or misguided understanding of socialism. Productive forces could only achieve limited development and at times were even at a standstill under this model of socialism.

China copied the Soviet model of socialist construction when it began to build socialism after the victory of its revolution. This was because China did not have any independent experience of its own at that time. Chinese leaders were also restricted in their concept of socialism by established Soviet ideas. Mao Zedong and other Chinese leaders raised doubts about this model and attempted to introduce reform, but they were unable to promote any reform in practice or, to put it another way, they failed to find the correct road to reform and made mistakes of a different nature.

Deng Xiaoping unequivocally stated in 1988, "... when we were copying the Soviet model of socialism we ran into many difficulties. We discovered that long ago, but we were never able to solve the problem."[1] He said in the previous year, "China is now carrying out a reform. There is no other solution for us. After several decades of practice it turned out that the old ways didn't work. We used to copy foreign models mechanically, which only hampered the development of our productive forces, induced ideological rigidity and kept the people

---

[1] Deng Xiaoping, *Selected Works*, Vol. III, p. 256.

and grass-roots units from taking any initiative."[1] He then pointed out that, "We made some mistakes of our own as well, such as the 'Great Leap Forward' and the 'cultural revolution,' which were our own inventions."[2] The "Great Leap Forward" and the "cultural revolution," were indeed China's unique creations; they represented misguided practices and, of course, were not powerful weapons for boycotting an inapplicable foreign model. The two basic drawbacks mentioned in points 1 and 2 above are also applicable to China.

The practice of copying a foreign model plus China's own mistakes had grave consequences. Deng Xiaoping said succinctly, "I would say that since 1957 our major mistakes have been 'Left' ones. The 'cultural revolution' was an ultra-Left mistake. In fact, during the 20 years from 1958 through 1978, China was hesitating, virtually at a standstill. There was little economic growth and not much of a rise in the standard of living. How could we go on like that without introducing reform?"[3] In contrast to traditional socialist concepts, Deng Xiaoping's thinking on reform lays stress on the following:

Firstly, Deng Xiaoping has stressed that we should proceed from the national realities in China and build socialism with Chinese characteristics, although traditional ideas represented by the former Soviet Union held that the existing socialist model was the most desirable and should be copied by every country.

Deng Xiaoping said, "This reform is part of the

---

[1] *Ibid.*, p. 321.
[2] *Ibid.*
[3] *Ibid.*

self-perfecting process of the socialist system, and in certain areas and to a certain extent it is also a revolutionary change. "[1] This is to say, on the one hand the reform is to be carried out within the socialist system, even though, to some extent, it is a revolutionary change; on the other hand the socialist system needs to be continuously perfected. This is in direct opposition to the traditional idea that once the socialist system was born it would be perfect, or only in need of a minor overhaul.

Secondly, Deng Xiaoping has stressed that we must promote productivity in socialist society through reform, and that the central task of reform is the development of productive forces. The first priority was therefore given to a shift in the focus of the Party's work after reforms were initiated in 1978. Deng Xiaoping said, "Since the Third Plenary Session of the Eleventh Central Committee, the Party has shifted the focus of all its work to the drive for socialist modernization and, while adhering to the Four Cardinal Principles, has concentrated on developing the productive forces. That was the most important thing we did to set things right. "[2]

Thirdly, Deng Xiaoping has stressed that reform also means the emancipation of productive forces. This view is in direct opposition to the traditional concept that only revolution leads to the emancipation of productive forces, and that there will no longer be the need to emancipate productive forces under socialism.

Here I would like to elaborate on the idea that reform also means the emancipation of productive forces.

---

[1] *Ibid.*, p. 145.
[2] *Ibid.*, p. 144.

A socialist society is established on the basis of the productive forces created by capitalist society, and capitalist society is negated during the process of the establishment of socialist society. The reason for this negation is that, with capitalist relations of production at the core, capitalist society can no longer promote the development of productive forces. The task of a socialist revolution is the freeing of productive forces from capitalist restraints. Will the need for the emancipation of productive forces still exist after a socialist society has been established? Will the task of emancipating productive forces remain? For a long period the answers to these questions remained negative throughout the world, although productive forces had developed slowly and even come to a standstill.

In the past, Mao Zedong tried to find a unique path. After the failure of the "Great Leap Forward" in 1958, he saw that socialist construction in China was not proceeding as rapidly as he had envisaged, and believed that there were still some obstacles to be cleared away. He was unsatisfied with merely copying the Soviet model, and tried to forge a new path. He did not make a comprehensive and scientific assessment of the failure of the "Great Leap Forward", but his attempt was not unwarranted. However, he failed to find the correct path because his assessment of the nature of the obstacles preventing the development of productive forces under socialism was completely wrong. He believed that the key to all problems lay in the fact that China had not carried the socialist revolution nor the struggle against the bourgeoisie and capitalism through to the end, and that the capitalist relations of production and the capitalist superstructure to a large extent still existed. He therefore argued that the task confronting us was to look for the bourgeois and capitalist evils in socialist society and struggle against them. This idea ran counter to objective reality and brought disaster in practice. According to this guiding principle, everything without the stamp of public or state ownership and every form of individual ownership were dangerous capitalist evils; every opposition to socialist concepts, even though dissention was minimal, was labelled capitalist, leading to disastrous consequences such as cutting off the "capitalist tail" in rural areas and the search for "capitalist roaders" within the Party. The concise expression of Mao Zedong's mistakes was "taking class struggle as the key link" and "the continuous revolution under the conditions of proletarian dictatorship". The latter slogan was not put forward by Mao Zedong himself, but gained his approval and conformed to his thinking. He believed that socialist productive forces could be developed only when they were continuously emancipated from capitalist shackles.

After the Third Plenary Session of the Eleventh Central Committee, the Party summed up its historical experience and came to the conclusion that class struggle was no longer the principal contradiction in China, although it still existed to a certain extent, and that the motive force for the development of socialist society was no longer class struggle, although the tendency to pull China back down the road to capitalism, i. e. , the tendency towards bourgeois liberalization, must be combatted. Restraints on the development of productive forces arise from an inappropriate socialist economic structure, which is related to mistaken concepts of socialism under given historical conditions, and not from capitalism.

Under such circumstances, trying to emancipate productive forces using revolutionary measures is like writing out the wrong prescription for an illness.

Deng Xiaoping emphasized that revolution means the emancipation of productive forces, and so does reform. He made a clear distinction between the tasks involved in the two forms of emancipation. He said, "The overthrow of the reactionary rule of imperialism, feudalism and bureaucrat-capitalism helped release the productive forces of the Chinese people. This was revolution, so revolution means the emancipation of productive forces. Now that the basic socialist system has been established, it is necessary to fundamentally change the economic structure that has hampered the development of the productive forces and to establish a vigorous socialist economic structure that will promote their development. This is reform, so reform also means the emancipation of the productive forces."[1]

The reform now needed by socialism in the process of its development is a fundamental change in the economic structure, which is linked to various rigid concepts and a structure that depends too much on centralized state power. Of course, this task cannot be accomplished by means of a so-called revolution against the bourgeoisie. Similarly, we cannot learn what is useful from foreign countries by "taking class struggle as the key link". Historical experience has shown that "taking class struggle as the key link" at home was closely connected to China's closed-door policy. Deng Xiaoping said, "The experience of the past thirty or so years has demonstrated that a closed-door policy would hinder

---

[1] *Ibid.*, p. 358.

construction and inhibit development. "[1] "To develop
its economy and shake off poverty and backwardness,
China must open to the outside world. "[2] He also said,
"The experience we have gained over the years shows
that with the former economic structure we cannot develop the productive forces. That is why we have been
drawing on some useful capitalist methods. "[3] It is not
a manifestation of weakness for socialism to draw on
useful capitalist methods; on the contrary, it shows that
socialism has great vitality. Of course, while keeping to
the policy of opening to the outside world, Deng Xiaoping has emphasized resisting all decadent capitalist tendencies.

The reform is part of the self-perfecting process of
the socialist system and therefore different from revolution by means of which one class overthrows another,
however, both emancipate productive forces. Deng Xiaoping said, "Just like our past revolutions, the reform is
designed to clear away the obstacles to the development
of the productive forces and to lift China out of poverty
and backwardness. In this sense, the reform may also
be called a revolutionary change. "[4] Since the history
of the traditional socialist structure and its deep-rooted
influence is decades long, it is not easy to break free either conceptually or in practice. The reform is therefore
revolutionary in terms of its depth and width.

Deng Xiaoping said, "We regard reform as a revolution — not as a 'cultural revolution' of course. "[5] He

---

[1] *Ibid.*, p. 74.
[2] *Ibid.*, p. 261.
[3] *Ibid.*, p. 152.
[4] *Ibid.*, p. 139.
[5] *Ibid.*, p. 89.

also said, "The reform we are now carrying out is very daring. But if we do not carry it out, it will be hard for us to make progress. Reform is China's second revolution. It is something very important that we have to undertake even though it involves risks."[1] Obviously, in his mind, the reform is completely different from the so-called "continuous revolution under the conditions of proletarian dictatorship" during the period of the "cultural revolution", although it too is a revolution. The reform is not simply an extension and continuation of the past revolution that has already achieved victory, therefore it is called the "second revolution" in China.

## IV.  A Socialist Market Economy

In the reality of life under socialism, the liberation of productive forces means shaking off the yoke of the highly centralized and all-embracing planned economy. Deng Xiaoping said, "We used to have a planned economy, but our experience over the years has proved that having a totally planned economy hampers the development of the productive forces to a certain extent."[2]

In the past, China always equated a socialist economy with a planned economy, believing that a socialist society could, and should, practice a planned economy. This was based on a misunderstanding of socialism, i. e. , since people have a high level of consciousness during socialist construction, we can know in advance details of production and economic activities and incorporate them into the plan. In fact, this is impossible. A

---

[ 1 ]  *Ibid.* , p. 119.
[ 2 ]  *Ibid.* , p. 151.

high level of consciousness is expressed in an understanding of the laws and directions of social development, but it is impossible to predict the details of all social and economic activities. When every place, every
social group, every enterprise, every production unit
and even every individual involved in economic activities
are required to act strictly according to the state plan,
initiative comes only from the central authorities, and
initiative from all other sources, especially from the
broad masses of workers, is stifled. Obviously, this is
contrary to the essence of socialism.

Deng Xiaoping sees these shortcomings of a planned
economy clearly and tries to bring into play the initiative
of all sectors of society. He said, "... experience has
taught us that we must no longer keep the country
closed to the outside world and that we must bring the
initiative of our people into full play. Hence our policies
of opening up and reform. "[1] He also said, "In a nut-
shell, our economic reform means invigorating the domestic economy and opening to the outside world. Invigorating the domestic economy means opening domesti-
cally, so as to stimulate the initiative of the people
throughout the country. As soon as the open policy was
implemented in the countryside, the initiative of the 800
million peasants was aroused. The open policy in the
cities will likewise stimulate the initiative of enterprises
and of all sectors of society. "[2]

Mao Zedong also saw the drawbacks and mistakes
of the planned economy in the Soviet Union in 1956,
when he initiated the basic policy of mobilizing all posi-

---

[1] *Ibid.*, p. 222.
[2] *Ibid.*, p. 139.

tive factors, internal and external, to serve the cause of socialism. No doubt this basic policy was correct. But how was it to be put into practice? In his later practice and theories, Mao Zedong resorted more and more to political means in implementing this policy. Methods such as "taking class struggle as the key link" and large-scale mobilization of the masses had grave consequences. Having learnt a lesson from this, Deng Xiaoping said in a speech delivered at the closing session of the Central Working Conference which made preparations for the Third Plenary Session of the Eleventh Central Committee, and took place not long after the introduction of the reform, "We must learn to manage the economy by economic means. If we ourselves don't know about advanced methods of management, we should learn from those who do, either at home or abroad."[1]

What are the economic methods that can overcome the shortcomings of a planned economy? These methods can by no means appear out of the void and must be sought in the historical experience of the development of human civilization. Deng Xiaoping said, "One way in which socialism [*socialism here obviously refers to the kind of socialism under which a planned economy prevails*] is superior to capitalism is that under socialism the people of the whole country can work as one and concentrate their strength on key projects. A shortcoming of socialism is that the market is not put to best use and the economy is too rigid. How should we handle the relation between planning and the market? If we handle

---

[1] Deng Xiaoping, *Selected Works* (1975—1982), p. 161.

it properly, it will help greatly to promote economic development, if we don't, things will go badly. "[1] While affirming the strong points of a socialist economy, this remark also points out its weaknesses, i. e., that it does not invigorate the economy and stifles the initiative of all sectors of society. Of all the articles in the *Selected Works of Deng Xiaoping*, this was the first to attach the foremost importance to the market and to point out the relationship between the economy and the market.

In traditional thinking, a market economy means private ownership and capitalism, and therefore it only exists in a capitalist society. Such an idea has been supported by generations of Marxists, and is also believed by the capitalist press and academic circles in the West. People believe that in order to resist capitalist influence, a socialist society must reject commodities and a market economy, and have a product economy under the control of national planning.

From a historical perspective, commodities and markets did not make their first appearance in capitalist society. However, it was in capitalist society, especially during the period of developed capitalism, that commodities began to encompass the whole of society, develop into a market economy, and further develop into a mature market economy. A developed market economy and all its mechanisms are the positive results of large-scale socialized production. Since socialist society is an entirely new society constructed on the basis of all cultures created throughout human history, it must draw on all the achievements of capitalism, including its tech-

---

[1]   Deng Xiaoping, *Selected Works*, Vol. III, pp. 26—27.

nology and methods of production, and the market economy that emerged with large-scale production. There is no reason to believe that socialist public ownership cannot accommodate a market economy linked to large-scale socialized production. However, traditionally a market economy was always rejected and this gave rise to the misunderstanding that a market economy only exists in capitalist society, and is necessarily related to privatization, and to the erroneous view that people can only choose either public ownership or a market economy, i.e., either socialism or a market economy, but cannot have both.

Generally speaking, all traditional socialist views after the October Revolution were that a market economy is incompatible with socialism because, in the opinion of the founders of Marxism, in future society would organize all productive and economic activities in a planned way, and there would be no exchange of commodities. However, a more important reason was that the major socialist countries were handicapped by their social and historical conditions. None of these countries had experienced developed capitalism. Before the revolution, commodities did not cover the whole of society and the structures of a market economy were not mature; after the revolution, with the heightened enthusiasm of the masses, an underdeveloped economy, small scale construction, and simple economic structures, the state was in a position to implement unified control and great achievements were made under a planned economy. However, such heightened enthusiasm could not last long if no fuel was added to the flames. With the development of the economy and an increasingly complex economic structure, the drawbacks of a planned economy became more and more apparent. Under these circumstances, if there was no fundamental reform of the planned economy and the advantages of a market economy were not acknowledged and drawn on, there would inevitably be not only a flagging economy, but also an unstable political situation.

From the time China entered the stage of socialism in 1956, a planned economy was practiced for more than two decades to the exclusion of a market economy. However, experience demonstrated that commodity production and the market could not be abolished. Economic conditions over these 20 or so years also revealed that when we accepted commodity production and respected the law of values we had more rapid economic development. Guided by "Leftist" ideas we did our utmost to reduce the range of commodity production, for example, we tried to turn the people's communes into self-sufficient units and to abolish rural market trading. We also tried to change the system of wages to a system of rations. In fact we were trying the impossible and moving backwards.

After the Third Session of the Eleventh Central Committee of the Communist Party of China convened at the end of 1978, a new period of Chinese economic development began. With reform of the economic structure, the scope of market regulation in both urban and rural economic life steadily broadened and the use of market mechanisms increased. At the same time, the scope of state plans, especially mandatory plans, was steadily reduced, with the result that the initiative in all sectors of society was brought more fully into play, the enthusiasm of the broad masses was aroused, and it became increasingly obvious that market mechanisms could play a basic role in the rational allocation of resources. In short, we can now do many things that could not be done under a planned economy. It is true that in the transition from a planned economy to a market economy numerous difficulties have been encountered, but the direction is clear and the road has been opened up.

Our policy is to maintain the predominance of public ownership and at the same time allow the proper development of various non-public economies, including the private economy. However, the introduction of a market economy does not mean that we practice privatization. The socialist market economy means maintaining the predominance of socialist public ownership, and bringing the positive role of a market economy into full play in order to promote the development of socialist productive forces.

The experience of market economies in the capitalist system has demonstrated that the state still has a role to play. The capitalist states also use macro-regulation to remedy the drawbacks and weaknesses of a market economy. A market economy under the socialist system will free the socialist state from the impossible responsibility for managing all economic activities at a micro level, and enable it to do a better job of economic macro-regulation in the interests of the working people and social development. Naturally, the state can also concentrate more resources on the work that must be undertaken by the state.

Based on historical experience, Deng Xiaoping pointed out that "There is no fundamental contradiction between socialism and a market economy. The problem is how to develop the productive forces more effectively. "[1]"Why do some people always insist that the market is capitalist and only planning is socialist? Actually they are both means of developing the productive forces. So long as they serve that purpose, we should make use of them. If they serve socialism, they are socialist; if they serve capitalism, they are capitalist. "[2] These two remarks were made by Deng Xiaoping in 1985 and 1987 respectively. In 1992, when he inspected the southern provinces, Deng Xiaoping said "The proportion of planning to market forces is not the essential difference between socialism and capitalism. A planned economy is not equivalent to socialism, because there is planning under capitalism too; a market economy is not capitalism, because there are markets under socialism too. Planning and market forces are both means of controlling economic activity. The essence of socialism is liberation and development of the productive forces, elimination of exploitation and polarization, and the ultimate achievement of prosperity for all. "[3]

In short, Deng Xiaoping has done away with blind faith in a planned economy and broken the taboos on a market economy. He has confirmed not only that socialism can use a market economy as a means of economic development, but that socialism should draw on all the experience of market economies accumulated under capitalism, which have helped boost large-scale socialized production and economic development, and make such experience serve socialism. This is one of the important

---

[1] *Ibid.*, p. 151.
[2] *Ibid.*, p. 203.
[3] *Ibid.*, p. 361.

contributions that Deng Xiaoping has made to the theory
of socialism.

(Written in March and April 1994 and
first published in *People's Daily*, 16
and 17 June 1994)

# Marxism Is a Developing Theory[1]

Marxist theory is in the process of continual development. This was pointed out by Engels a long time ago. In 1887 he said in a letter to an American lady: "Our theory is a theory of evolution, not a dogma to be learned by heart and to be repeated mechanically."[2] And from this point of view, Engels once warned that, "... one might expect fixed, cut-to-measure, once and for all applicable definitions," but this is a "false assumption."[3]

What makes Marxism scientific is that facts are taken as the final criterion, and it steadfastly upholds the integration of theory and practice. This characteristic of Marxism dictates that theory can and must always develop in tandem with the development of actual life.

To say that Marxism is a developing science is not to say that the basic tenets of Marxism are unstable. The basic scientific theory which Marx and Engels developed in the mid 19th century and the period thereafter

---

[1] A speech at the opening of the Theoretical Seminar on Studying *Selected Works of Deng Xiaoping* and the Theory of Building Socialism with Chinese Characteristics on 24 December 1994.

[2] "Engels to Florence Kelley-Wischnewetzky in New York," in Marx and Engels, *Selected Correspondence*, Moscow: Progress Publishers, 3rd edition, 1975, p. 378.

[3] Karl Marx, *Capital* vol. 3, Moscow, Foreign Languages Publishing House, 1959, p. 13.

from the standpoint of the most advanced class of workers was a summary of man's historical experience. This
theory was shown to be correct by later social practice.
These basic tenets include: a world view and a historical
perspective based on man's scientific knowledge of nature and his experience of socio-historical development;
penetrating and comprehensive analysis of the capitalist
economy and society that was reaching maturity in some
Western countries at the time, which led to the theory
that in the course of its development capitalist society
would be replaced by socialist society; and the theory of
the establishment of a working class political party capable of shouldering the task of socialist revolution.

The value of these basic principles lies in the fact
that they can be effectively applied to reality. When
people in later times applied these principles, naturally
they had to begin from the actual historical conditions in
which they were placed. Therefore, the basic principles
of Marxism are of necessity continually replenished and
enriched by human society's new experiences and new
knowledge; otherwise Marxism would become a fos-
silized dogma.

Hence, we cannot restrict Marxism to the things
that Marx (or Engels, or perhaps their great disciple
Lenin) said. We cannot judge whether something is or is
not Marxism simply on the basis of whether the
founders of Marxism said it or not.

Marx died in 1883, and Engels in 1895. Between
the latter part of the 19th century and the present,
mankind's knowledge of nature and the history of human society have gone through enormous changes and
developments. The concrete aspects and course of these
changes and developments have been such that the

founders of Marxism could not have predicted them, nor did they attempt to predict them. As the 20th century rapidly draws to a close, if we take a look back at these developments and changes, we may feel that the developments made in Marxism so far are not compatible with the developments of modern life. Therefore, we perhaps feel that the development of Marxism is a task that every sincere Marxist should shoulder.

## I

The soaring developments in science and technology over the past hundred years have provided a phenomenal breakthrough for human society.

The founders of Marxism paid close attention to research into the natural sciences and the development of science and technology. There were two reasons for this: Firstly, a dialectical and materialist view of the world must be firmly based on a scientific knowledge of nature. Secondly, the development of the forces of production plays a decisive role in social progress, and as the history of society approaches closer to modern times, the role of science and technology in the forces of production becomes more and more important.

Marx was proficient in mathematics, and in the course of his studies of political economy he also delved deeply into related subjects such as chemistry, agricultural chemistry, biology, and geology. In his later years he became very interested in experiments designed to create cells using chemical synthesis. Marx was also keenly interested in all aspects of the application of electricity, and recognized that the invention of the long-distance electric cable, which he saw in 1882, had great potential. Engels had a profound understanding of every branch of the natural sciences. In a speech at Marx's grave he said: "Science was for Marx a historically dynamic, revolutionary force. However great the joy with which he welcomed a new discovery in some theoretical science whose practical application perhaps was as yet quite impossible to envisage, he experienced quite another kind of joy when the discovery involved immediate revolutionary changes in industry, and in historical development in general."[1] As we can see, in Marx and Engels' time the applications of electricity could only just be glimpsed. Although Engels died somewhat later than Marx, the motor car only appeared in the year of his death. At that time, the most modern means of transportation used on a worldwide basis were railways and steamships. As far as science and technology are concerned, the 20th century presents a very different aspect.

Following the advancement of the forces of social production with the invention of the electric generator, the electric motor, and the internal combustion engine at the end of the 19th century, science and technology in the 20th century have made great strides towards a new stage. The revolution in physics at the beginning of this century signalled the arrival of a new scientific era. Since the 1940s, developments in science and technology, such as nuclear energy, the electronic computer, automation, space flight, satellite telecommunications, electronic information technology, and bio-engineering,

---

[1] Frederick Engels, "Speech at the Graveside of Karl Marx," in Marx and Engels, *Selected Works*, Vol. 3, Moscow, Progress Press, 1970, pp. 162-63.

have opened up new fields of production, creating hitherto unimagined possibilities for the development of the
forces of production, and giving rise to a revolution in
many aspects of human social life. It is completely appropriate to describe the developments in science and
technology in the second half of the 20th century as having advanced by leaps and bounds. During this period,
the new developments and creations of each decade have
outnumbered those of the past 2,000 years. In developed countries, the time from the creation of a new
technological item to its practical application is also get-
ting shorter by the day.

By relying on science and technology, countries that
have begun to develop in the 20th century can often
reach an economic growth rate that would have been impossible in the last century, and catch up with countries
previously in the front rank. Science and technology
constitute a productive force that is most dynamic. This
point has become clearer during the past few decades
than during any previous age.

The development of science and technology increases man's knowledge of the natural world, both macro-
scopically and microscopically, inorganically and organi-
cally, to an unprecedented level. New knowledge does
not negate Marxist materialism or its dialectical world-
view, but rather reinforces this world-view. Using
man's new knowledge of the natural world to enrich the
Marxist world-view should be the duty of contemporary
Marxists.

Marxism is by no means a type of sectarianism,
since in the course of its formation, Marxism absorbed
all the valuable achievements made in the history of human society, especially those created by man in a capi-

talist system. This absorption did not come to a halt once Marxist doctrines had been formulated; Marxism cannot afford to overlook any of the achievements of modern science if it wishes to develop. In fact, one could say that it is unimaginable to attempt to develop Marxism without them.

The contemporary development of science and technology, while creating the potential for rapid development of the forces of social production, has at the same time brought with it many problems for capitalist society. These problems affect education, employment, communications, the structure of industry, natural resources, ecology and environmental protection, and other areas. Socialist society also has to face these problems. On the one hand, progress in science and technology can bring benefits to the inhabitants of the globe, but on the other, in the modern world the proportion of poor and half-starved people who live in under-developed countries is constantly increasing. These contradictions, which exist because of and are produced by the capitalist system, cannot be solved by the development of science and technology alone. There is absolutely no doubt that Marxism, if it is to develop, must face these problems.

The development of science and technology must inevitably have a massive impact on the question of how capitalist society can enter the stage of socialist society, and how those countries which have already set up socialist systems can construct socialism. That is, in considering these questions, we must take into account the historical conditions in which science and technology are making their rapid advance. A particularly obvious fact is that if the advanced capitalist countries monopolize ad-

vanced science and technology, then a victory for socialism would be out of the question. Therefore, as far as
constructing socialism is concerned, it becomes a press-
ing task to fall more closely in step with the tide of scientific and technological development, so as to give full
play to the superiority which socialism should and can
achieve.

## II

In the one hundred years since the deaths of Marx
and Engels, the Marxist socialist ideal has become a reality in vast areas of the world. But there are two historical phenomena which demand attention. One is that socialism, unlike the situation envisaged by Marx and Engels, was not born first in the most advanced capitalist
countries, but in countries in which capitalism had not
developed far or in particularly backward countries. The
other is that, following the establishment of socialist
systems in some countries, they could not be sustained
for long. In the Soviet Union, which was a major nation, they sang the song of victory for socialism; now
they are singing a dirge.

The question of whether or not socialism will first
appear in advanced capitalist countries is, of course, a
question of whether or not the capitalist system will be
the first to crumble. In 1891, four years before his
death, Engels said in a letter to Bebel: "You said that I
had prophesied the collapse of bourgeois society in 1898.
There is a slight error there somewhere. All I said was
that we might possibly come to power by 1898. If this
does *not* happen, the old bourgeois society might still
vegetate on for a while, so long as a shove from outside

does not bring the whole ramshackle old building crashing down. A rotten old casing like this can survive its inner essential death for a few decades, if the atmosphere is undisturbed. So I should be very cautious about prophesying such a thing. "[1]

World War I broke out twenty years after Engels' death, and some thirty years later there was a severe economic crisis which rocked capitalism. Fifty years after Engels' death another war broke out even more ferocious than World War I. Historical facts demonstrate that the Marxist theory that contradictions exist in capitalism which cannot be solved by capitalism alone is sound, but, on the other hand, they also show that the great capitalist edifice is not easy to topple. In fact, the major capitalist countries are still in existence a century after Engels' death and look set to continue for quite a few years to come. Today's Marxists must admit the truth of the first fact and should conduct a thorough going analysis of the second on the following premise. The frenzied development of the forces of social production, far from accelerating the breakdown of the capitalist edifice, is providing the capitalist ruling class with the materials to shore it up. However, the unbalanced development of capitalism accelerates the process of the rise and decline of the major powers, and exacerbates the contradictions within the capitalist world. By analyzing these facts and predicting the future course of capitalism, a new perspective can be added to the theoretical arsenal of Marxism.

During the 1960s, a controversy arose in the ranks

---

[1] "Engels to Bebel," in Marx and Engels, *Correspondence of Marx and Engels*, New York, International Publishers, 1942, p. 492.

of international communism over whether or not a peaceful transition was possible, but neither side in the debate proved sufficiently persuasive. The prophesy that "wars bring about revolutions or revolutions prevent wars," based on the experience of the first and second world wars, is unrealistic, at least for the foreseeable future. Perhaps it was the case that the alternatives of peaceful transition or armed struggle were too simple; history cannot mechanically repeat itself. This should help people to liberate their thinking and, starting from reality, conduct new theoretical investigations.

The founders of Marxism postulated that socialism could be triumphant in a comparatively backward country, but it would follow a particular road. When Marx pondered over the question of the Russian agricultural communes in 1881, he suggested that these communes could avoid going through the "Caudine Forks of the capitalist system," that is, "take advantage of all the positive achievements of the latter [*capitalist system*] without passing through all its dreadful vicissitudes."[1] But this would only happen when the Western proletariat were victorious. An article signed jointly by Marx and Engels put it this way:"If the Russian revolution becomes the signal for a proletarian revolution in the West, so that both complement each other, the present Russian common ownership of land may serve as the starting point for a Communist development."[2]

---

[1]  Karl Marx, "First Draft of the Reply to V. I. Zasulich's Letter," in Marx and Engels, *Selected Works*, Vol. 3, Moscow, Progresss Publishers, 1970, p. 153.

[2]  "Preface to the Russian Edition of 1882," in Karl Marx and Frederick Engels, *Manifesto of the Communist Party*, Beijing, Foreign Languages Press, 1975, p. 6.

However, a situation in which revolutions in the East and West act as signals to each other and supplement each other has never come about. On the contrary, historical experience has shown that, whether or not revolution succeeds in a country, the type of victory achieved and the way in which the country proceeds along the road to socialism greatly depends on the conditions in that country. External conditions can only play a partial and secondary role. Disregarding a country's conditions and "trying to make plants grow by tugging at them" will always result in failure. Viewpoints which overemphasize international influence are always contradicted by real life.

There are facts to prove that not every country has to traverse the whole course of capitalist society, and "go through the Caudine Forks of the capitalist system". However, it is clear that if the country does not go through this "fork," the new society must go through various interim stages in place of all the fearful twists and turns of capitalism; it cannot march directly to a victorious and mature socialist system. This is something that those in the last century could not have foreseen.

According to Marx's discussion of this problem, unless the maximum rate of development of the productive forces of social labor is guaranteed, we cannot enjoy all the positive achievements of the capitalist system, the foremost of which is clearly modern production power, and therefore we cannot speak of transcending the "Caudine Forks of the capitalist system". This basic viewpoint should be supported.

# III

From the 1920s onwards, people began to face the questions of how to establish a socialist system and how to carry out socialist construction following the victory of a socialist revolution. The Marxist arsenal has no ready-made answers to these questions. In a review of the first volume of *Capital*, Engels wrote, "But as for what is going to happen after the social revolution—on that he gives us only *very* dark hints."[1]That was naturally all he could do, because actual life at that time had not posed such questions, nor had it supplied the materials necessary for their scientific investigation.

In the 20th century Marxism has gone from being a science of revolution to a science, not only of revolution, but also of construction. The task of revolution is far from complete worldwide. The science of revolution also requires creative development. The science of construction needs to be established from the ground up. Since socialism requires the setting up of a brand-new society different from all previous societies, we could say that the science of socialist construction is the science of revolution. But the questions it poses are related to the establishment of a new society, not the overthrow of an old society. Therefore, it cannot be restricted to the original science of revolution. Running a country and setting in motion a revolution are different in nature. The duties to society of an oppressed political par-

---

[1] Engels' Review of vol. 1 of *Capital* for the *Düsseldorfer Zeitung*, see Karl Marx and Frederick Engels, *Collected Works* (New York; International Publishers, 1985). p. 216.

ty in a country ruled by an exploiting class and a political party in power in a socialist country are clearly different. Revolution breaks out in a society in turmoil, while construction needs social stability. Under these two different sets of historical conditions the function of class struggle and its concrete manifestation are of course vastly different. Marxism focussed on a study of the historical experience of previous societies, but research from the perspective of construction, compared to that from the angle of revolution, requires that attention be paid to many hitherto neglected areas. Scientific analysis of old societies is helpful in establishing new societies, but constructing new societies must be based on new experiences.

There are certain patterns common to socialist revolutions in different countries, but the actual course of the revolutions and their concrete forms are by no means stereotyped. Each country must tread its own path to socialism based on its own national conditions. In terms of constructing socialism, although the ancient Chinese referred to the ideal society of the future as "great uniformity (大同)," it seems that one cannot simply look at the "uniformity" and ignore the "differences". In other words, "uniformity" can only be attained through "differences". Each country must decide its own specific road and specific methods for socialist construction based on its historical conditions, national cultural traditions, economic and social development, and its position in the global configuration. History has already shown that attempting to make different countries conform to a uniform model is impossible.

The construction of socialism in capitalist countries with a high level of productive forces must entail a number of problems; these problems are even more complex in relation to the construction of socialism in countries where capitalism is less developed or undeveloped.

Over the past seventy years, mankind has acquired considerable experience in socialist construction, including both its success and failure. In the task of the overall transformation of the old world and the construction of a new world setbacks and failures are inevitable. Engels put it well when he said, "the proletariat, like all other parties, becomes clever most rapidly through its own mistakes which it can never be completely spared of."[1]

The collapse of socialism in the Soviet Union and the countries of Eastern Europe in the early 1990s was the greatest failure ever encountered in the history of the communist movement. This failure testifies to the fact that the science of socialist construction is far from mature. In the field of construction, Marxists must eliminate the various mental shackles that hinder people from seeking truth from facts, summarize their experiences, and initiate a new situation. In this way, such a failure can provide the ideological initiative for advanced people to construct a new world.

An important duty for contemporary Marxists is the summarizing of the successes and failures in the construction of socialism this century, especially the failures, in order that they may develop the science of socialist development as part of Marxism.

---

[1] *Collected Works of Karl Marx and Frederick Engels.* Vol. 37, Berlin, Dietz Verlag, 1967, p. 327.

# IV

Chinese Communists have made an unremitting effort to develop Marxism in China, and have been very successful.

In the course of the democratic revolution, Chinese Marxists opposed the prevalent theory that China was a special case, i. e. , that China's national conditions were absolutely unique and thus Marxist class analysis, and the theories of class struggle, social development, and scientific socialism were inapplicable to China. Dogmatism, which mainly sprang from inside the Party, was also opposed because it did not take into consideration China's actual conditions, and even alienated people from Marxism. Those dogmatists who regarded Marxist ideas simply as items from a book and ready-formed foreign experiences did not understand that even if they were guiding principles applicable to China, they still had to harmonize with China's concrete reality before they could be useful to the nation. They also failed to understand that foreign experiences, even if successful, could not be applied indiscriminately to China. Triumphing over these two erroneous tendencies, the Chinese Communists, in the course of long practice during the Chinese democratic revolution, upheld and developed Marxism. The Chinese Communists, with Mao Zedong as their representative, based their revolutionary practice on the facts that China was a semi-colonial, semi-feudal nation, that the development of capitalism was weak, and that peasants constituted the overwhelming majority of the population. They produced revolutionary theories with Chinese characteristics, establishing rural revolutionary bases, arming the peasants under the leadership of the proletariat, and using the country-side to surround the cities. This path was heresy to the dogmatists, but practice proved that under China's historical conditions it was a creative development of Marxism, which resulted in a victory for the Chinese revolution that the dogmatists had no faith in.

The democratic revolution under the leadership of the Chinese Communist Party only discovered the true road to victory after experiencing defeat. The situation is the same as far as the problem of socialist construction is concerned. Although many achievements were made in the construction of socialism in China in the twenty years following 1956, it did not develop rapidly, and there were many setbacks and failures. Experience has therefore shown that, firstly, the indiscriminate application of the Soviet model failed to solve China's problems. It was perfectly all right to learn from the Soviet Union in circumstances in which China lacked experience, but such information should have been used mainly for reference and on a selective basis, especially since the Soviet model itself contained fatal flaws. Secondly, the indiscriminate application of the actual experiences of class struggle and the mass movements of the revolutionary period did considerable harm. It is true that the good experiences and fine traditions of the revolutionary period must be carried on, but it is impermissible to apply them indiscriminately while disregarding concrete changes in the situation. The great victory of the Chinese revolution gave the methods which led to that victory enormous prestige. In a situation in which China itself had no new experiences, and was unwilling to copy the experiences of other countries, this led quite easily to a search for the road to socialist construction based on the concrete experience of the victory of the democratic revolution, and to the use of abstract concepts related to socialism to explain these experiences. Practice has shown that this way of doing things could not solve the problems of socialist construction.

The Chinese communists, with Comrade Deng Xiaoping as their representative, have, step by step, formulated a theory of socialism with Chinese characteristics, based on a summary of a China's own successes and failures in construction, and with reference to the experience of other countries. The Third Plenary Session of the Eleventh Central Committee of the Chinese Communist Party, held in December 1978, was of epoch-making significance. Following this, various policies and other measures were put into effect, centering on economic construction, and firm support for the party leadership, socialism, and reform and opening to the outside world. In the past decade or so the construction of socialism in China has taken on an entirely new look. It has achieved tremendous victories and remained firm as a rock through all the storms and turmoil of the world. Practice has shown that the theory and methods of building socialism with Chinese characteristics are great developments of the Marxist theory of Socialist construction under Chinese conditions.

Of course, we are a long way from being able to say that socialist construction is complete, nor can we say that we have fully formulated the theory of socialism with Chinese characteristics. Several decades of hard work are still required and various difficulties have still to be overcome before we arrive at a complete victory for socialist construction. We still need to engage in practice and immerse ourselves in scientific study of the theory of building socialism with Chinese characteristics, so as to make clear a number of laws which have never before been elucidated. The world in which China finds itself is one in which science and technology are developing rapidly, and in which dramatic political and economic changes are taking place. Chinese Marxists must acquire accurate knowledge of the world and understand the relationship between China and the rest of the world.

To do this, we must liberate our thinking, seek truth from facts, and always begin from reality. We must uphold and develop Marxism.

(Written in 9 December 1994. First published in People's Daily, 27 December 1994.)

# Several Problems Related to the Study of China's Modern History

## —Preface to the Second Edition of From the Opium War to the May Fourth Movement

In November and December 1995, when I was away from work to recuperate, I picked up *From the Opium War to the May Fourth Movement* which I had written at the beginning of 1980 and which was published in 1981. This was the first time I had read the book from cover to cover since it came off the press.

In the process of reading the book and making corrections and amendments I thought over several problems related to the study of China's modern history, and would like to use this opportunity to express what was in my mind. The first problem is related to classes and class struggle. In writing my book I adopted the viewpoint and method of class analysis. This was not because I had to maintain a Marxist position, but because I believed that only by adopting the Marxist viewpoint and method of class analysis could I clearly express the historical problems with which I was dealing.

The book is a political history covering the first half of China's semi-feudal, semi-colonial period, that is, from 1840 to 1919. After more than 2,000 years of stagnant feudal society, China plunged into unprecedented social and political turbulence and change. During that period of time, on the whole, the old classes remained although they were in decline; new classes had emerged but they had not yet been victorious. The class struggle of the past therefore survived, while class struggle in the new era was in the making. The infiltration of imperialist influence made the internal contradictions and struggles between the classes in China more complex. The conflicts between China and the imperialists involved class as well as national issues, because different classes in China had different attitudes towards the foreign aggressors. Although of course their attitudes were not immutable. If we overlook these points we end up with only a description of historical phenomena and are unable to make things clear. If I had written a general instead of a political history I would not have departed from this viewpoint and method.

Of course, one should not attribute every social phenomenon to class and class struggle, nor play up any social contradiction as one between antagonistic classes or between one class and another. The simplistic and formulaic Marxist viewpoint of class analysis is not a desirable approach.

There have been many revolutions in the course of China's modern history and almost all have taken the form of armed struggle—the highest form of class struggle. The revolutions referred to here are those events that involved the overthrow of the old ruling class and changed the old social and political systems.

My views on these revolutions expressed in the book have attracted diametrically opposed comments: Some say my opinion of them was too low while others say I had a too high opinion. From the very beginning there have been different views on these revolutions. Relatively speaking, there is less disagreement over the 1911 Revolution, but opinions still vary widely. In my view, standing on a higher historical plane and pointing out the weaknesses of the 1911 Revolution and the reasons for its failure to achieve greater success is not to deny its historical status and significance. Outright rejection of the Revolution is of long standing; its earliest proponents in academic circles were KangYouwei（康有为）and Liang Qichao, who raised repeated objections to the Revolution even before it broke out and, after 1911, condemned it on the grounds of the turmoil it would leave in its wake.

In my opinion, any revolution that goes along with the historical tide of class struggle should be considered necessary and conducive to social progress, even if it is neither mature nor successful, and has serious shortcomings and many negative effects.

Some people consider reform a better approach than revolution and therefore one should not worship the latter. However, history bears witness to the fact that in terms of social and political development revolution only occurs when the road to reform had been blocked. We should not make an abstract assessment of any revolution or reform without taking into account the specific historical conditions in which it takes place. In my book, the terms reform and reformism refer to the steps and methods employed to push forward social progress. Reformism played a positive role in the fight against the old forces and became a vanguard in the revolution. However, it has also played a negative role in negating revolution, and as a result has often had a dual nature in China's modern history. When a revolutionary situation arose and the flames of revolution began to rage, if the reformists had not changed their stand with the times, the spearhead of their struggle would have been aimed at the revolution rather than the old forces. Moreover, the old forces would have made use of the reformists in their struggle against the revolution.

After China entered the socialist period, radical changes took place in the social and historical conditions. Of course there should have been great or even radical changes in the concepts of class, class struggle and revolution in accordance with the actual conditions. Although contradictions between classes still exist in the primary stage of socialism, they no longer constitute the major social contradiction. Now that the nature of such social contradictions has changed, different methods should be used to resolve them.

When we say that reform, opening to the outside world and enlivening the economy are also a form of revolution, it is clear that the meaning of revolution in this context is different from its meaning in the past. The experience gained from solving contradictions between classes, in class struggle and revolution in the past remains significant today, but such experience should not be applied purely mechanically to our current tasks. Experience has shown that it is completely wrong to take class struggle as the key link in resolving social and political problems during the socialist period. We must proceed from the realities of the primary stage of socialism in order to gain a clear understanding of the trends in various classes and strata, and the differences between them and the classes in the old society (in some respects there may appear to be no difference in form), and to devise new ways and means of coping with and re-.

solving class and other social contradictions.

The second problem is related to opening to the outside world. China has pursued a policy of opening to the outside world since the Third Session of the Eleventh Central Committee of the Communist Party of China (CPC) and its door is opening increasingly wide. Economic, technical and cultural exchanges with foreign countries are increasing, and China has gained experience in using funds from abroad and in using foreign markets and resources. This, although still limited, represents a completely new phenomenon in Chinese history.

Why do we say that the experience is completely new? Because in the past, apart from commercial and cultural exchanges with foreign countries in ancient times, China had isolated itself from other countries, and only opened its doors to the world in the one hundred years after the Opium War as a semi-colonial nation.

During this century or more, some foreign funds were indeed brought into China but almost all the funds were extorted from the country itself; the imperialist nations placed their capital in China only to intensify their exploitation and oppression, and to impede the development of Chinese national industries. The volume of foreign trade in that period was very small, exports consisted mainly of agricultural and mineral goods, while imports consisted of manufactured items. Opening-up of that kind could do nothing more than keep China poor and backward. Although the imperialist nations forced China to open her doors wide so that they could pass through them without hinderance, China's opening to the outside world was in fact at a very low level, since this type of opening reduced China to even greater poverty and made it impossible for her to expand her contacts with foreign countries. At that time, no one dared to dream of using foreign capital, markets and resources to develop China's own economy.

In 1944, shortly before the end of the War of Resistance Against Japan, when people had begun to speculate about China's future after the war, I read in an article in a periodical published in the Kuomintang area that foreign countries should help China to become strong and prosperous, and that only a stronger China could significantly expand its trade and economic exchanges with foreign countries, which would be of benefit to all. To reinforce his argument, the author noted the volume of trade between the United States, the nations of Western Europe, and Japan before the war, and compared such trade with that between these countries and China. The latter was pathetically small.

This article impressed me very much; after so many years I have forgotten the names of both the journal and the author but I clearly remember his argument, which at the time I thought not unreasonable. However, it was wishful thinking to believe that such arguments would persuade the imperialist nations to allow China to gain genuine independence, or to help China grow strong and prosperous. The consistent policy of the imperialist nations was that, on the one hand, they wanted to keep China's doors open but, on the other, they oppressed China and kept China poor and backward. As a result, China opened its doors only marginally, and it could even be said that there was no real opening-up to speak of. This contradiction could not be resolved by relying on imperialism. Only when the Chinese people won complete national independence through their own efforts, and, by relying on their own strength, began to develop their economy in accordance with the specific conditions in the country could this contradiction be resolved.

It is precisely because of the fact that China's efforts to implement a policy of opening to the outside world as an independent state over the last decade or so are so completely new that we cannot use past experiences to interpret the new phenomena. Likewise we should not use new experiences to reinterpret historical phenomena during China's semi-colonial period, and dismiss existing knowledge about that period as antiquated and incorrect.

The Open Door Policy for China proposed by the American government in 1899 and 1900 was absolutely different from China's current opening to the outside world. At that time, the imperialist powers had divided their spheres of influence in China. The so-called Open Door Policy of the United States implied that the sphere of influence of each imperialist power in China should be accessible to all imperialist powers alike. While I discussed the problem of opening up in both *From the Opium War to the May Fourth Movement* and in *Imperialism and Chinese Politics*, I naturally could not make a comparison with current practices.

The third problem relates to whether or not it is possible to take modernization as a theme when narrating or discussing the modern history of China. This book was published a little more than a year after the epoch-making Third Plenary Session of the Eleventh Central Committee of the CPC, when the "cultural revolution" and the practice of taking class struggle as the key link were being categorically repudiated. As a result, some of those in history circles felt that it was not appropriate to place too much emphasis on class and class struggle. It may have been because of this consideration that the idea arose of taking modernization as the theme when writing about modern history.

In spite of this, no books based on this idea have been written (or perhaps they have been published but I, being ill-informed, have not heard of them). However, I believe the idea is workable. The efforts made by generations of Chinese people since the Opium War of 1840, the twists and turns they have taken, the difficulties and hardships they have experienced, and their differences and disputes, are all important topics in the history of modern China. Obviously it is of great significance to use them as subjects when writing the modern history of China.

However, taking modernization as the thread of modern Chinese history does not necessarily mean that the viewpoint and method of class analysis should be excluded. On the contrary, if the viewpoint and method of class analysis are not used, it will be very difficult to interpret and resolve many complex problems in relation to the modernization drive in modern history.

In the history of modern China, modernization has involved industrialization and the resultant changes in economic, political and cultural areas. Modernization in China from the late 19th century to the early 20th century meant the realization of capitalism, and at that time the question of socialism had not yet been placed on the agenda. Capitalism in China was a question of the conflicts or balance between various internal social forces. However, it was not merely an internal problem, since the aggressive imperialist forces had already penetrated

China. It could be said that the earliest force driving China towards a limited degree of modernization was none other than imperialism. The reason I say a limited degree of modernization is that, wherever they reach in the world, the imperialist powers invariably seek to transform nations and countries into their own image. However, they do not like them to be as powerful as themselves, and only allow them to develop in the direction of capitalism to an extent that favors their colonial rule.

The colonies that won national independence after World War II are obvious examples. They had long been under colonial rule, in some cases for as long as three or four hundred years. During the period of colonial rule, the imperialist rulers decided the destiny of the colonies and the colonial people. In their own interests the imperialist rulers intentionally retained all the pre-capitalist social relations that hindered national progress and development. Capitalism developed, but only within certain limits and only to the advantage of the imperialist rulers and a handful of local people. All of these colonies, without exception, were poor and backward when they became independent. In a considerable number of areas where capitalism was fully developed the indigenous people were almost wiped out. Some people have gone as far as to suggest that if China had been a colony for decades then modernization would have been achieved. This is preposterous!

After the aggressive forces of foreign capitalism expanded into China following the Opium Wars, it was impossible for Chinese feudal society to remain intact. The imperialist powers would not allow China to adopt a closed-door policy and remain unchanged.

The imperialist oppression also stimulated the Chinese people to search for a new path. Under such circumstances, modernization in modern Chinese history inevitably involved two approaches: One was modernization within the limits allowed by imperialism, that is, the feudal social and economic system and its political and ideological superstructure were to be maintained and changes were to be made only in some aspects and to a limited extent in order to draw China closer to capitalism; the other approach was to breakdown the limits imposed by imperialism and strive for national independence and then modernization.

These two approaches were quite different in modern Chinese history, but sometimes they were so confused that they could not be distinguished from each other. A great deal of effort has been expended in distinguishing between the bureaucrats of the Westernization Movement and the bourgeois reformists of the 1860s to the 1890s, the former being representatives of the first approach and the latter the vanguard of the second.

When we talk about opening to the outside world, we must differentiate between the opening that took place under colonial or semi-colonial conditions, and that in an independent state. Likewise, when we talk about modernization, we also must differentiate between the modernization that occurred within the limits of imperialism and that based on maintaining independence and keeping the initiative. In my opinion it is impossible to define the differences between the two approaches or to clarify various questions related to modernization if we depart from the Marxist view and analysis of class.

I discussed the above problems in my book, although not in detail. I wrote in the past few years some articles on these topics and I will have a few excerpts from these articles to be appended to this preface for reference of the readers.

Lastly, I would like to make reference to a few problems.

Firstly, some readers and friends suggest that I should write another book covering the period from the May Fourth Movement to the founding of the People's Republic of China. As a matter of fact, I have considered this but I have not yet begun. Perhaps my age and health will not allow me to finish the writing. I want to entrust the work to some of my friends.

Secondly, all the references to the quotations in the first printing of the book refer to source materials published before that year. I rechecked some of the quotations against source materials published after 1981 when this book was later reprinted, while other quotations were not rechecked. The style was therefore not consistent. This is still the case with this edition.

Thirdly, there is a biographical index in the first edition (made by my friend Sun Jieren, who passed away two years ago). I and many of my readers find it very useful. Using this index it is easy to find details of a particular person and events related to him. The original names of Europeans and Americans can also be easily found in this index. Of course, it would be even better if there was also an index of events. I make special reference to the index here because there is usually no such index in Chinese academic works.

(Written at the end of December 1995;
revised 25 August 1996)

# China's Role in the 21st Century*

Will China be a stabilizing and positive force in Asia and in the world in the 21st century? I believe an affirmative answer can be given. The following are my views on this issue.

A retrospective of the out-going 20th century shows that the situation in China in the second half of the century was very different from that in the first half. During the first half of the 20th century, China suffered from poverty, weakness and internal disintegration, and was subject to the bullying and humiliation of the world powers. China was then an extremely unstable factor, without an independent position in the international community. The imperialist powers battled with one another and even resorted to war in their scramble for greater interests in China. The Japanese militarists attempted to annex China by force and once occupied half of the country. China became the major battlefield in the Far East during World War II. In the second half of the 20th century, the situation was completely different. With the victory of the Chinese revolution and the founding of the People's Republic of China in 1949, Chi-

---

* This speech was delivered by Hu Sheng at the lunch meeting of first conference of the 21st Century Forum, held from 4-6 September 1996 in Beijing and sponsored by the National Committee of the Chinese People's Political Consultative Conference.

na achieved independence and internal unity, gaining the capacity for self-defense and self-development. It has neither begged a living from others nor allowed other ·countries to trample upon it at their will. Gone are the days when international disputes were caused by the so-called "China problem".

Even now certain forces in some countries still hold the belief that it would be in their interests to cause the disintegration of China and reduce the country, which is heading towards prosperity and strength, once again to poverty. However, we can only draw one conclusion from our experiences in the 20th century. China is located at the eastern end of the Eurasian continent and the western Pacific coast and has a vast territory and a large population. If the country was divided, weak and poor, it would not only bring misery to its own people, but would also become a destabilizing factor and a burden to the world, and would play a negative role in peace and development.

In terms of prospects for the 21st century, China should continue to do what it has endeavored to do in the second half of the 20th century, to play a more positive and stabilizing role in promoting peace and development in the world. To reach this end, China should first ensure that its people, who account for one fifth of the world's population, have enough food and a fairly comfortable life; and, secondly, China should have the self-defence capacity necessary to let the world know that the country brooks no invasion or plundering. If China fails to achieve these two goals there might be an unprecedentedly large flood of refugees, or international rivalry over China. Either of these possibilities would lead to major international disasters.

During the last two decades of the 20th century, China has focused its efforts on the socialist modernization drive and continued its reforms and open-door policy. During this twenty-year period, China's economy has grown at an average annual rate of approximately 9%. Experience has shown that economic development in China has benefitted both the Chinese people and those countries that have economic links with China. It seems certain that this momentum of development will continue in the 21st century. Any external force that tries to contain this developmental momentum will be unjustified and doomed to failure.

Some research institutions across the world believe that China's economic aggregate will be one of the largest in the world during the first two decades of the next century. Even if this prediction comes true, China will still be a developing country if calculations are made in per capita terms. China's self-defence capability will increase, although there will remain a large gap when compared to the major powers of the world. Deng Xiaoping maintains that China will reach the level of moderately developed nations by the 2050s. Many statesmen and scholars believe that this forecast can be realized, although it will require painstaking efforts. By this time, China could possibly be called a powerful and prosperous country. It therefore follows that the possibility of China being a destabilizing factor in the world because of its poverty and weakness can be ruled out. However, some may raise another question: Will China definitely be a stabilizing and positive force in the world when it reaches the point of being a major prosperous and powerful country?

Based on historical experiences, it is generally be-

lieved that regional and world orders always undergo
change and adjustment when a new power rises. What
impact do such adjustments and changes have on international relations? Is it positive or negative? It seems to
depend, to a great extent, on the systems and policies
adopted by the emerging power.

China is a socialist country and has adopted a socialist system. The socialist system with Chinese characteristics has won the approval and support of the majority
of the Chinese, including those who do not have a special liking for the socialist system, since in practice this
system has enabled the people to lead a better life year
by year, and has made the country more prosperous and
powerful. There is no reason to think that the Chinese
people will not march forward along this path in the 21st
century. The question we must now answer is: Can the
socialist system practiced in China and the various policies derived from this system guarantee that the country
will continue as a stabilizing and positive force in the
world during the next century?

There have been different social systems in the history of mankind. At the beginning of the 20th century,
the capitalist system prevailed in or ruled almost the
whole world. The socialist system, which was considered able to eliminate the evils of the capitalist system,
was once only an ideal held by many people of various
nations. However, after the first decade of the 20th century, this ideal gradually became reality in some countries. Capitalist and socialist systems thus co-existed and
both experienced many harsh trials.

In the 20th century, especially during the later period, developed countries of the capitalist world made
positive contributions of far-reaching significance to

mankind with their major advancements in science and technology. Yet, on the other hand, the rise and fall of the major capitalist powers and the oppression of small, weak nations by the great powers were the root cause of turbulence and instability in the international situation. The two world wars, which brought the most severe trauma to people across the world, stemmed from the capitalist system rather than the socialist system. The system whereby suzerain states forced many poor, weak and underdeveloped countries to become their colonies had completely collapsed by the latter half of the 20th century. The colonial system could no longer be tolerated and was forced to withdraw from the arena of history.

Judging by its overall achievements in the 20th century, although the socialist system did not develop by plundering other countries as the capitalist system did, it does have major weaknesses. The first socialist country in the world was a major force in achieving victory in the anti-fascist war, and made great contributions to mankind, yet its domestic and foreign policies can hardly be regarded as sound or in conformity with socialist ideals. Some are even contrary to socialist ideals. A glaring example is the way in which other socialist countries were treated in a chauvinist manner and reduced to the status of satellite states. It even resorted to arms to maintain this structure. The socialist banner collapsed in the first socialist country, followed by other socialist states like falling dominoes. This demonstrated at the very least the lack of vitality of this type of socialist system. Military confrontations and the arms race between the East and the West since the 1950s have consumed massive amounts of resources on both sides. This was one of the reasons for the dramatic changes in some Eastern countries.

These facts have prompted some observers to suggest that the 20th century was one in which socialism went from its birth to its demise. It is, however, too early to say this. It is true that it might have been difficult to refute such judgments if there were no nations like China or others that still uphold the socialist system. The history of the progress of human society shows that a new-born social system cannot develop soundly without undergoing many setbacks and failures. It should be said that mankind has accumulated rich experience with regard to socialism in the 20th century. In light of their experience in this regard people can see how socialism was distorted and, if such distortions are not corrected, socialism cannot develop well. People may also understand what should be done and what should not be done in the construction of socialism.

The historical experience gained in the 20th century does not testify to the extinction of socialism, but it does demonstrate that the socialist system needs reform. The socialist model that prevailed throughout most of the 20th century is not the one and only possible model. As the end of this century approaches, new models are ushering in the revival of socialism. The Chinese Communists represented by Deng Xiaoping have succeeded in generating new plans for the socialist cause in China in the late 20th century, since we have learnt a great deal from our successes and failures, particularly from our failures. New creations are hardly possible without lessons drawn from these failures.

China will continue to adhere to the renovated socialist system suited to Chinese conditions during the

21st century. This system demands that the focus of the country's endeavors should be economic development, and the objective of economic development should be the improvement of people's living standards. A socialist market economy is the objective of economic restructuring, and improvements in and expansion of socialist political democracy while developing the economy. With regard to opening to the outside world, this demands exchanges and cooperation with all countries in the fields of economics, trade, technology, etc., on the basis of equality and mutual benefit. To practice such a system, we need a peaceful international environment and we must carry out a foreign policy of peace.

China is now pursuing its foreign policies in conformity with the nature of its socialist system, which are, *inter alia*, not to seek hegemony or be a super-power, but to oppose hegemonism and power politics in any form; to handle relations between states according to the five principles of peaceful coexistence, with non-interference in each other's internal affairs at the core; maintaining that the social system and way of life of a country are to be decided by its own people; advocation of the complete equality of all countries, large or small, promoting democracy in international relations; and, calling for a peaceful solution to international disputes. Some of these policy principles were put forward in the early days. During the process of China's socialist modernization drive, we have no wiser choice than to stick to and further improve these policies in our external relations.

We are now talking about China in the 21st century, and issues related to the next one or two generations. Of course, we cannot stipulate what our descendants should do. They have to make their own decisions according to the development of the situation. But history should not be cut off. The experience provided by China and other countries in socialist construction in the 20th century is very important. They have made the latest contribution to the great treasury-house of experience gained during the progress of human society. The conclusions drawn from experience will surely be respected by our descendants, who will know from that on the road to prosperity and strength, if China fails to be a stabilizing and positive force in the world, the nation will be in danger of self-destruction. The experience we have gained will teach them how to ensure the sound development of socialism in China, and how to make sure that China plays a stabilizing and positive role in the world, and makes its due contribution to world peace and development.

**图书在版编目(CIP)数据**

关于中国发展道路的思考:胡绳的九篇论文:1983~1996:
英文/胡绳著. —北京:商务印书馆,1997.3
ISBN 7-100-02447-1

Ⅰ.关… Ⅱ.胡… Ⅲ.社会主义建设模式-研究-中国-文集-
英文 Ⅳ.D61-53

中国版本图书馆 CIP 数据核字(97)第 03146 号

GUĀNYÚ ZHŌNGGUÓ FĀZHĂN DÀOLÙ DE SĪKĂO:
HÚSHÉNG DE JIŬPIĀN LÙNWÉN

关于中国发展道路的思考
胡绳的九篇论文
(1983—1996)
胡 绳 著

商 务 印 书 馆 出 版
(北京王府井大街 36 号 邮政编码 100710)
新华书店总店北京发行所发行
一 二 〇 一 印 刷 厂 印 刷
ISBN 7-100-02447-1/K·527

1997 年 4 月第 1 版 　　开本 850×1168 1/32
1997 年 4 月北京第 1 次印刷 　字数 184 千
印数 1500 册 　　　　　印张 6⅝ 插页 1
定价:18.00 元